FILM

FILM FUEL

THE — LIFE-CHANGING FILM FUNDING SECRET

JOSIAH STENDEL

Cover design by Yago Domingues
Interior design by Megan Sheer

CONTENTS

PART 1: A NOTE TO THE STARVING ARTIST

PART 2: FROM MOVIE TO MOVEMENT

PART 3: GOT FUEL?

DEDICATION

To the starving artists among us—
the desperate directors,
penniless producers,
and flat-broke film students.
Let's end this funding famine.

PART 1

A NOTE TO THE STARVING ARTIST

1| FILM FUNDING REIMAGINED

"If you want to make movies, go make a movie."
GREAT. VERY HELPFUL. BUT WHERE DO I GET FUNDING?

"Just work with what you've got."
RIGHT. BUT WHAT ABOUT EQUIPMENT? LOCATIONS? CAST AND CREW?

"Real filmmakers max out their credit cards and pay with exposure!"
ARE YOU SURE YOU'RE DOING THIS RIGHT?

You probably encountered the starving artist dilemma early in your filmmaking career. Like me, you realized a need for proper funding to make better movies. Since then, you've tried producers, film festivals, crowdfunding, and all the other presumed paths into Hollywood. I don't know about you, but none of those led *me* to films with real budgets.

You know what worked?

Forging a different path. Blazing a fresh trail. In doing so, I acquired *$75,000 for a simple short film* and unlocked a waterfall of funding opportunities—more than enough for me. In fact, the FilmFuel approach is so bountiful I want to invite you to experience the fruits of this film-production-promised-land for yourself.

What if I told you there was a way to fund your film without begging your friends or selling yourself into slavery? You keep all the equity in your work and retain complete creative freedom. It's a system that doesn't require any startup money, that you can set into motion right now, and that works regardless of your location. The icing on the cake? This approach inherently leaves a financial footprint on a social cause near to your heart. If this sounds like heaven (cue angelic chorus), you're holding the silver bullet.

Read religiously. Apply immediately.

Now, I'm guessing this isn't your first rodeo.

Perhaps you've participated in film funding workshops before, subscribed to newsletters and YouTube channels that promised answers, or even read other books and articles on the subject. I'm not here to keep you from trying any of those things. But if you've given them a go and left burnt-out or disappointed, it's not your fault. If you've been unsuccessful in getting films funded in the past, maybe with a failed Kickstarter campaign or hunt for producers, please hear me—it's not your fault.

The internet boasts a wealth of knowledge. Although it can be a blessing, misinformation and half-truths quickly get confusing. Information overload can paralyze you from taking even the tiniest steps toward success. It's okay.

If you're worried that the cards are stacked against you, that you can't succeed with fueling your films, I want to take a second and put those fears to rest.

ONCE AND FOR ALL. YOU CAN DO THIS!

You just need the right person to explain it to you.

The big studios say you need A-list talent and hotshot producers with access to hundreds of millions in funding to be successful. I'm here to tell you that they're wrong. Studios propagated the myth that short films and indie features can't make money. They have reasons for wanting you to think that, but it's simply not true anymore. If you've ever thought that the entertainment industry *wants* you to fail, you're probably right. They don't benefit from your films being successful and taking away attention from their blockbuster releases.

But as an independent filmmaker myself, I believe in you and care about your success. That's why I'm writing this. You live and breathe movies. It's your calling and obsession. You dream of making a difference with the stories you were born to tell, and I want to make that happen.

I want you fully funded—making your movies your way.

My goal with FilmFuel is to equip a new generation of filmmakers to *power their films by empowering others*.

If you reduced this entire book to one equation, that would be it: Movie + Movement = Momentum.

MOVIE + MOVEMENT = MOMENTUM

Suppose I handed you a blank check and asked you to fill in the dollar amount your film needed. What would you write? Get a specific number in mind. If your desired budget is a hundred grand or less, you will learn all you need to get fully-fueled traction to rival movies with ten times the resources.

But what if your number is higher? Perhaps multiple six, seven, or even eight figures. In that case, I will help you channel FilmFuel *in conjunction with traditional strategies* to maximize your impact and multiply your funding.

If you haven't heard my name before, you're probably wondering, "*New book, who dis?*"

I'm a filmmaker and marketer with well over a billion video views to my name. I've worked on breakout television hits like *The Chosen*[*] and some

---

[*] Which also happens to be the #1 highest crowdfunded media project in history. Check out www.thechosen.tv to learn more and to stream the critically acclaimed episodes for free.

of the most successful YouTube channels of all time. But when I started making films with friends, my biggest struggle was finding funding.

In fact, I remember my movies by all the ways I *failed* to fund them.

My first production was a disastrous foray into crowdfunding. Without so much as a home movie to my name, I set myself a lofty goal of several grand and smashed the big red launch button. Thirty days later, my campaign came to an unceremonious end. I hadn't even raised enough to buy a roll of gaff tape. It became clear that relying on sheer goodwill to fund my films wasn't sustainable unless I already had a massive following.

Next, I tried grants. Although I applied to a whole mess of them and even collaborated with professional grant writers, not a single organization acknowledged my submission. It honestly felt like throwing my time into a black hole.

The industry told me to search for investment at film festivals. Like others, I was drawn in by pointless ego-boost awards only to discover that my self-funded film screened in a room nobody visited.* By all means, shoot for Sundance and Cannes. The right events can be both prestigious and valuable networking opportunities. But I learned first-hand that too many film festivals are moneymakers advertised as celebrations of local art. Others are downright scams. Dozens of festivals—and nearly $2,000—later, I still had no funding. In fact, besides a few rinky-dink laurels and awards, I had nothing to show for the money I burned.

Desperate, I pivoted into the world of filmmaking contests. These competitions temptingly promise six figures in cash and gear as prizes. However, after several disheartening near-misses, I realized I might as well be playing the lottery. Although certain fundamentals set good films apart from great ones, the judging is—by definition—subjective. Sure, there's a slight chance of winning the resources to make your films. But counting entirely on the luck of the draw to supply your film is risky. Unnecessarily risky.

---

* In my research, I interviewed a director who premiered a self-funded film at a tiny festival in Tampa, Florida. The one person who attended the screening walked over afterwards, introduced himself as a producer, and essentially wrote a five-figure check on the spot. It can happen, but film-festival-Cinderella-stories like this are exceptionally rare.

What happens if you don't win?

Will your movie stay a script for another year?

I even dipped my toe into the world of independent film producers. Believe it or not, I was contacted by a self-made millionaire from Los Angeles who expressed intentions of investing in my film. However, as unnecessary delays turned weeks into months, I realized I was at his mercy. He wanted substantial plot changes. He pushed off production dates once. Then again.

He finally canceled the shoot and shelved the project entirely.

The empty promises of this well-intentioned, wanna-be investor made life difficult for my team, who graciously scheduled my film around other commitments. Although I smoothed things over to the best of my ability, the experience could easily have ruined my reputation.

At this point, I had given everything the ol' college try, and I was still as broke as before. Except now, I was broke *and* frustrated. Something had to give if I was gonna make another film.

Maybe you've been in a similar situation.

One day, I caught an interview with a Hollywood filmmaker, and something big caught my attention. Studio productions receive a significant portion of funding from corporations.[*]

"*Huh,*" I thought. "*I should try that.*"

But after countless doors slammed in my face, I finally called it quits. Local businesses weren't interested in funding my big ideas. And why should they be? They're worried about the bottom line, and it didn't benefit them to help me.

But in that *dark night of the soul,* I had my epiphany.

"What if I make this project about *helping others* and use my film about orphaned brothers to raise money and awareness for orphaned children? Maybe businesses could get behind that?" After my previous funding flops, I honestly wasn't expecting much. With this new plan, however, the difference was immediate. The first approach resulted in more money for

---

[*] Traditionally, this looks like product placement, but the business world is taking an increasing interest in the entertainment industry. For example, did you know that several major hedge funds invest in Hollywood films?

my film than all of my past attempts *combined.* Within days, my short film was fully supplied and fully funded. I ended up with well over $75,000 in resources committed to this project—cast, crew, equipment, catering, locations, and yes—even cold, hard cash.

For a *short film!*

At this point, fireworks and signal flares started going off in my mind. *This actually worked!*

My breakthrough seemed illogical. After all, how can giving away money help you make more? But after the funds started rolling in, I realized the truth. I had stumbled upon a brilliant way to power my film by empowering others. In the years that followed, I started figuring out what made this work and why. Eventually, I refined this technique into a step-by-step process that would make funding *any* film infinitely easier.

And the benefits of the method persisted long after production wrapped. That one short film got a team of forty dedicated professionals behind it. It opened doors for us to host a red-carpet premiere for over six hundred raving fans and inspired several television and newspaper interviews. We even secured nationwide distribution on DVD and streaming platforms. Ultimately, the film raised thousands for orphaned children across America.

Don't believe me? Search for *Orphaned Courage* on your favorite streaming platforms or grab a limited-edition DVD to see the film and join the movement. Yes, that was my shameless plug.

Perhaps even more insane, I was six-freaking-teen at the time. Wait, wait! I'm not fishing for compliments. I simply want to prove that if I could do this, literally *anybody* can. Your film probably isn't about orphaned brothers, but attaching a movement to your movie still applies, no matter the plot. Let me explain.

Here's how to fund a low-budget film the traditional way.

Your first option? Put in overtime at your day job for the next ten years.* Better get comfortable eating instant ramen in your parent's basement because you'll need every penny for that mythical production budget. Or

---

* This is not hyperbole. I know multiple indie filmmakers who spent a decade or more scrimping and saving to self-fund their first films.

you could launch a crowdfunding campaign and watch your friend circle shrink. After begging enough people, *someone* might feel sorry enough to throw you a bone. If all else fails, give Dave Ramsey nightmares. Shoot the thing on plastic! Max out every credit card and go hundreds of thousands of dollars into debt. I hope you hear some snark and disdain in the above suggestions. These options are neither fun nor sustainable.

In the echelons of larger budgets, the prospects are just as painful. Within the Hollywood system, a minimum-wage producer's assistant will toss your script onto a mile-high stack of other hopefuls—never to be read, seen, or made. On an indie level, you'll likely wind up with glorified washing machine salesmen as "producers," running and ruining your show. Sound familiar?

But what about established methods like pre-sales, deferred payment, gap financing, and the like? **Pre-sales** sounds appealing on the surface. You sell a distributor your dream. In exchange for the rights to your future movie, they cut you a check to fund production—yay, money! What nobody tells you is how rare deals like this are today. Without famous faces attached and a budget in the millions, pre-selling your film is a pipe dream.

Gee, thanks, man. If I knew Leonardo DiCaprio, do you really think I'd need this book?

As opposed to upfront compensation, **deferred payment** puts off paying your team **until after** your film is made. The idea is a nice **one: you** pay them out of future box office **earnings.** When your movie makes money, they **do too.** In practice, however, things look less rosy.

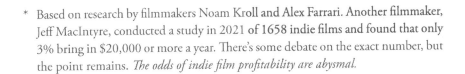

LESS THAN THREE PERCENT OF INDIE FILMS MAKE A PROFIT.[*]

---

[*] Based on research by filmmakers Noam Kroll and Alex Farrari. Another filmmaker, Jeff MacIntyre, conducted a study in 2021 of 1658 indie films and found that only 3% bring in $20,000 or more a year. There's some debate on the exact number, but the point remains. *The odds of indie film profitability are abysmal.*

Congratulations. You just made your crew a promise you can't keep. Those who actually care about your work? *Burned.* Will they trust you again next time? *Not a chance.* I have personally witnessed this tragic scenario more times than I can count.

Gap financing is a loan against future earnings of your film to "bridge the gap" between making the movie and making money. It's another high-risk, credit-card-esque situation where you spend the money before you make it. If the film doesn't generate enough money to repay the loan—and we've already established those odds are nonexistent—you are personally responsible for the balance. Bummer.

Some filmmakers distribute **equity backend points** in exchange for funding. This involves awarding your team and investors "points" representing portions of your film's ownership and future earnings. It might not cost you anything now, but it leaves you with minimal upside if your film *does* earn something or is picked up for distribution. For most indie films, equity is worthless, and potential collaborators know this.

Another common option is **Fiscal Sponsorship**, the process of legally "borrowing" the tax-exempt status of a non-profit organization. This qualifies you for hundreds of grants and even government funding. Which sounds great, right? But it comes at a cost. Fiscal Sponsorship means lots of red tape and loss of creative freedom. More on this later.

The punchline? Every method I've listed makes turning a profit on an indie level ridiculously difficult. Don't get me wrong. Difficult doesn't mean impossible. But even if you're wildly successful, it can feel like everyone makes money except for you.

The most likely outcome? Nobody makes money, and you're left taking the L. As with anything, there are exceptions. Sometimes the filmmaker ends up in the black. And rarely, one or the other breaks through to become a Hollywood darling. But do you want to bank your career and financial future on those odds? I don't know about you, but it bothers me that these processes don't do right by filmmakers—the ones pouring blood, sweat, and tears into each film. The system is flawed. The more money you raise, the more freedom you have to give up. You essentially sell yourself into slavery to contributors and creditors.

The FilmFuel method described in this book makes film funding accessible and sustainable. Before long, you'll be fueling your dreams and, at the same time, a charity of your choice.

"Attaching a cause sounds cool, Josiah—and, sure, I'd love to give back—but I don't even have the cash to fund my own dream, let alone somebody else's!"

We'll discuss this in-depth soon. For now, know that different entities (let's call them Fuelers) are much more willing to contribute finances, food, locations, and equipment to your film when you have a purpose backing it up.

By the end of the book, you will have the spark of an evergreen support structure. Why evergreen? In contrast to "one-time help" from a grant or contest, this system will keep supplying funds as long as you keep making films. In addition, you never relinquish creative control or intellectual property rights. The beauty of that is the ability to create passive income. We're talking royalty checks from streaming platforms, rolling in for every project you make for years after you've made the film. Imagine the peace of mind when this is all set up.

Maybe you're asking yourself if attaching a cause will work for *your* film. The answer is YES. This strategy still applies, even if it's a slasher flick or a sci-fi piece.

Before we explore how to greenlight your movie with FilmFuel, I want you to take a simple first step. Remember I asked you what amount you would write on a blank check for your film's budget? I want you to take out your checkbook. Yes, right now. Do this with me.

Write a fresh check to yourself in the amount of your desired budget. The number should be big enough to scare you a little bit.

Then add your film's title in the memo line.

Place this check in your wallet or hang it where you'll see it daily. It should serve as a constant reminder until the day you can 'date' it and cash it in. That's the

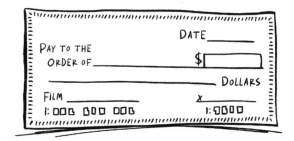

day your film will be fully funded. I know it may feel silly or insignificant, but I want you to do it. C'mon. Commit.

Now that you've got a goal, we can start moving towards it. Ready to explore what FilmFuel can do for your film? Then what are you waiting for—flip that page like it's hot.

2| THE STRUGGLE

What would you say is the number one struggle independent filmmakers face? Is it building their production team? Finding quality talent? Writing a script worth producing?

In 2016, I completed my 30-minute action short, *Orphaned Courage,* with an insane amount of support from the local filmmaking community. Two years later, as I revisited photographs from production week, I became overwhelmed with gratitude.

On a whim, I pulled out my phone and started typing up a simple social media post. I asked independent filmmakers to share the challenges they faced in the comments. Perhaps there was an introduction they needed. Or maybe I could guide them past obstacles using previous experiences. I felt indebted to them and wanted to help.

The response was overwhelming. Although more than one thousand two hundred filmmakers replied, the common denominator was a single issue:

>	» "Our biggest struggle? Budget, budget, budget."
>	» "Hands down, financing."
>	» "Getting money is our biggest struggle right now."
>	» "Money. I don't want people to feel like they're just doing us a favor or being exploited."
>	» "Funds. Always."

You get the idea. Out of the 1200+ responses, I could trace roughly 90% of all filmmaking challenges back to a lack of proper funding. For example, several filmmakers lamented their lack of access to equipment. Having the financial means to rent or purchase necessary gear would fix this, right? Another recurring issue was the lack of a dedicated team. Instead, many admitted they relied on a fully-volunteer cast and crew who often weren't very committed. Funds sufficient to hire experienced crewmembers would also remedy this issue.

Please don't misunderstand.

More money is not a magical fix-all solution. Clever filmmakers rely on creative solutions (not financial ones) to solve their problems. In fact, I would argue that embracing your limitations is the key to unlocking real creativity.

There is no better example of this than my dear friends Elliot and Zander Weaver, creators of the indie masterpiece *Cosmos*. Their modest $7,000 film budget is absurdly low for even the simplest of features, let alone for an ambitious science-fiction spectacle. Understandably, a budget so low came with intense challenges and compromise. But the ingenious way these brothers embraced their limitations ultimately led to international distribution and worldwide acclaim.

Creating a no-budget feature wasn't always the plan, though. The original vision, a film called *Encounter*, needed millions in outside funding.

"Your concept and team are great," investors told them, "but you don't have a bankable track record. You've made commercials and music videos, but feature films are different."

Pitch after pitch ended the same way. Without investment.

"It was really frustrating," Zander laughs, remembering the early rejections. "But after getting the same feedback so often, you have no choice but to listen."

Instead of shelving the project or waiting for their big break, the brothers pivoted. In full Robert Rodriguez mode, they focused on available resources and re-wrote the script to take full advantage of them. This meant simplifying locations, cast and crew, and equipment requirements. Easier said than done.

With a story set in a car at night, the two brothers decided to convert a friend's garage into a soundstage. Instead of a pricey cinema rig, the brothers used a $600 camera and a cheap lens off of Amazon. They now routinely get asked if the film was shot on an Arri Alexa. Taking advantage of the camera's tiny form-factor, the brothers mounted the camera inside the car, getting shots that would not have been possible with a larger rig. No dolly? No problem. They repurposed an old wheelchair for the task—the brother with the camera, seated, and the other pushing. Outside of these humble gear expenditures, the rest of the budget went to gas, food, and the electricity bill.

What's the punch-line?

RESOURCEFULNESS TRUMPS RESOURCES. ALWAYS.

You can't outspend your problems. At the same time, *you need the right tools to get the job done.*

After all, you wouldn't dig a hydroelectric dam with a garden spade, right? You need massive cranes, excavators, and more to pull off that kind of construction. Unfortunately, the right tools are often prohibitively expensive. Even with the democratization of the filmmaking industry, we still find ourselves hitting the glass ceiling of limited resources.

Or put another way, there are only so many favors to cash in before you need to *put* cash in.

After my informal research, I realized finding funding wasn't just a *me* problem. It plagued the entire filmmaking industry. From that moment on, I became obsessed with creating a solution. Then I remembered the funding process I developed on *Orphaned Courage.*

Could this be the answer?

Like any respectable American, I grabbed a stack of sticky notes and brainstormed until my wall looked like a patchwork investigation board in the home of a nutty conspiracy theorist. By the year's end, every inch of that room was covered in scribbles and pinned-up notebook pages. After the dust settled, I had something sustainable, repeatable, and scalable to any size budget. I had FilmFuel.

Before we dive into the specifics of developing a cause to attach to your film, I need you to first understand what you're getting yourself into. I know you're a creative person. All this business stuff is probably the last thing you want to think about.

Have you noticed? Artists have the weirdest relationship with money.

On one hand, we need it to survive. And there never seems to be enough of it. On the other hand, we see art as a higher calling. Something no money could pay for. If financial success were our primary objective, we'd be in a different line of work.

So, if taking money for your art feels like you're selling out, try a simple mindset shift. View each dollar for what it is—a thank you note from a viewer you entertained, informed, or inspired. Their payment to you is their display of gratitude. Business isn't bad, and money doesn't have to be icky. In fact, in the coming chapters, you'll discover how money from your art can create an impact that outlives you.

If you're pursuing a filmmaking career, you've got to embrace it as equal parts art and business. That's the bottom line. And that's why you're here! I'll do my best to keep everything super relevant and practical so that you can spend as little time as possible funding and as much time as possible filming. Deal?

3| WILL I GET RICH QUICK?

Solutions that promise immediate or short-term gains are very rarely the real deal. Success requires sustained effort. FilmFuel is not for people who want to put in a dollar today and get a million out tomorrow. That's not how this works. This methodology is a long-term solution that will set you up for success for years to come, but it requires commitment and leg work on your part.

I won't sugarcoat it. It will take time and effort. But with this book to guide you every step of the way, getting fully funded will finally be within reach.

PLEASE HOLD FOR THE OBLIGATORY FINE PRINT...

There's no way I can legally guarantee results of any kind. It wouldn't be fair. I don't know you, your personality, or your work ethic. Every situation is different, and your success is ultimately in your own hands. However, with this book, I'm handing you all the tools and tactics I used to generate nearly six-figure support for my short film. I'm laying it all out for you. Everything you need to transform your filmmaking career. *Adios, starving artist!*

But whether you choose to put these strategies into action or not is up to you. In my experience, there are only two types of people: those who take action and get funded and those who make excuses. You can't be both.

The good news is that right here, right now, you get to choose. Which are you going to be?

4 | WHAT KIND OF FILMS IS THIS FOR?

This process is also not for A-list studio filmmakers. If this book were my childhood bedroom, it'd have a "*No Big-Shot Studioz Allowed!*" sign taped to the door. Although budgets of any size can adopt FilmFuel, this process likely won't be as practical for those needing $200 million to make their next blockbuster.

Well, that's only half true.

In Chapter 56, we'll explore practical ways to tweak the FilmFuel process for super-sized budgets. But really, this process is best suited for the multitasking, many-hat-wearing independent filmmaker. Maybe you're both directing and producing and need a practical approach to funding, promoting, and launching your films.

I mean, most of us would benefit tremendously from an additional $10-50K for our short films, right? Or an extra $100K-1M for our features? YES! Absolutely, we would. And it's much more attainable than you might think.

This methodology will grow with you and your career. For example, starting with short films now, graduating to features in the future, and perhaps one day getting your foot in the Hollywood door to make that

$200 million studio blockbuster. Whatever your path or destination, these strategies will guide and accelerate you from start to finish.

What Genres?

Cause-driven films before FilmFuel have almost exclusively been documentaries, so you may be wondering if this approach has genre limitations. Let me assure you, every type of film is fair game. Even monster movies.*

Although it is true that documentaries will have an edge, FilmFuel was originally designed with narrative films in mind. Whether your film is a documentary, drama, comedy, romance, action, science fiction, fantasy, or horror film—following this process will get you funded.

But will it turn my film into a public service announcement? Don't worry. Even if you don't think your storyline is redemptive, the right cause is already lurking in your script somewhere. We'll find it. No script changes required. I have yet to find a story that doesn't have FilmFuel potential.

Short Films Too?

There's a reigning myth in the filmmaking industry that *only feature films make money.* Although that may have been true decades ago, the arrival of the internet changed the game completely.

Shorter-form content and episodic material have taken the world by storm.

I successfully validated this premise with *Orphaned Courage.* In fact, would you believe that I'm *still* receiving royalty checks each quarter from this thirty-minute film? If you know what you're doing, you can create a living with reliable, passive income streams from well-produced, short-form content.

---

* Don't believe me? Check out the Appendix for a full list of genres and a few cause ideas for each.

What If I'm a Young Filmmaker?

If you're a young filmmaker and feel looked down upon because of your age, this book will free you. Trust me; I know the feeling. I was there when I started this, remember?

As a young filmmaker, I thought I couldn't get any traction or funding. I thought Fuelers wouldn't take me seriously.

But I was wrong. And as you'll soon see, you can build insane momentum riding solely on the fact that you're a young filmmaker. If you're a high-schooler or film student wanting to pull off a movie that requires more money or resources than you have, stick with me. These strategies apply to you too. Age is no longer a drawback if you approach FilmFuel the right way.

5| FINDING FUNDING

Earlier, we explored the typical funding options presented to the independent filmmaker and their fundamental flaws. Whichever path you choose, there were only two likely outcomes. The movie almost certainly won't get made if you decide to wait on a big break. Alternatively, if you push through without the proper funds, you either compromise your vision or find yourself in deep debt. And the filmmakers who end up pulling everything together under budget often launch their films to the sound of crickets. They've put in all that work, but nobody cares enough to watch it! If you don't have the privilege of going into pre-production greenlit and fully funded, that's often the sad reality of independent filmmaking.

FilmFuel is a complete inversion of the system.

It revolves around attaching a cause to your project—perhaps assisting adoptions, benefitting people with PTSD, or supporting an animal shelter. There are dozens of nuances and tricks to help you leverage this approach into a fully-funded film, but it's ultimately that simple.

THE SECRET TO FINDING FUNDING IS CONNECTING A MOVIE TO A MOVEMENT.

When you link your work to a social cause, you'll suddenly find take-my-money support from those previously ignoring you. Your film becomes meaningful, something Fuelers can get behind. Not only do you get to make your movie bigger than imagined, but you're also left with funds to fulfill the advertised purpose of the film—giving back to others. Ultimately, making a difference with your work leads to your sustainable success.

Why Commit to FilmFuel

Why does FilmFuel outshine the other options? Many reasons. It works for projects of any size. Even short films can turn a profit with this strategy. In addition, FilmFuel puts an end to badgering others for money.

We've all got that friend who only reaches out when they need something, right? I've been that friend. Everyone assumes your coffee invite has a hidden agenda. Yuck.

FilmFuel doesn't exclude your friend circle but instead lets them open up their network to you. Instead of asking for cash, you instead ask them for introductions. Friends connect you with *others* (primarily businesses) who have fuel to add to your fire.

But wait, there's more. What if your film became *magnetic* to the top talent around? A mission-driven film attracts committed cast and crew. By creating a project your team believes in, FilmFuel produces an unquenchable desire in them. They want to make this happen. Even on a tiny budget! If you try to stop this train, watch out. Your team might carry on the crusade without you. If you're a young filmmaker who's tired of not being taken seriously, get ready to experience the hands-down best solution for student film funding.

The best part about FilmFuel? It's evergreen. Instead of a one-time boost to your filmmaking career, such as a grant or contest would be, the FilmFuel framework sets you up for repeated success. Just tweak, rinse, and repeat.

FilmFuel turns the power structure of the film industry on its head. You are no longer beholden to the Hollywood filmmaking mecca. FilmFuel can be effectively implemented *anywhere*—downtown LA or small-town USA. Now *you* can have the leverage, the power to greenlight your film. What could be more independent?

6 | IS THIS LEGAL?

Connecting your film to a cause is the crux of the FilmFuel method. But perhaps, red flags are going off in your mind. *We link a movie to a charity for our benefit? Isn't that fraudulent?*

No, FilmFuel is the real deal.

What *would* be fraudulent is approaching businesses and making them *think* we are a charity by soliciting "donations." Charities are separate, tax-exempt entities set up with the government and subject to all sorts of regulations. Starting a charity is great, but that's not what we're doing here. Fuelers are not donors. Framing their contributions as "donations" would be fraudulent unless we are a registered non-profit organization.

The other potential pitfall would be declaring the giving of proceeds to charity when the money, in reality, goes into your own pocket. This would be a flat-out lie, which is also not what we're doing here. Either of these approaches would be wrong, unethical, and illegal on many levels.

Bad, bad, bad. Please never do that. Pinky promise?

Instead, when we state that a portion of our film's profits will be given to charity, that is exactly what we do. Contributing to charity with the success of your project is an integral part of FilmFuel. Well, that begs the question. Why attach a cause at all?

YOU CONNECT A CHARITY TO THE PROJECT AS YOUR MOMENTUM MULTIPLIER.

Think about it this way. Film funding through traditional means is like pushing your film uphill. Demanding and miserable.

FilmFuel flips it.

When you attach a social cause, you experience crazy acceleration. It's as if your film is rolling downhill, picking up speed, and snowballing to epic proportions. Instead of calling in favors to secure cast and crew, they're calling *you*. Instead of begging people for help, now Fuelers are *looking* for ways to help you. What you get out of FilmFuel is massive forward momentum for your movie. More and more opportunities. More and more traction.

7| TURNING MOMENTUM INTO MONEY

BUT JOSIAH, HOW CAN I MAKE MONEY IF I GIVE IT ALL TO CHARITY? HOW WILL THAT FUND MY FILM?

Attaching a cause gives Fuelers a reason to support your film. Their contributions will become your film's budget. Those coffers are for production, though, and not for you. What will pay and sustain you? The film's *profits*. By following the FilmFuel monetization strategy, you can legitimately generate profits while contributing to charity.

But before I take you deeper, I need to lay some groundwork.

Although in developing FilmFuel, I have consulted with over a dozen attorneys and accountants, I am not an attorney or financial professional. I ask you to please do your due diligence before applying any of these strategies to your projects. As disclaimed at the start of this book, the ideas, suggestions, and techniques described in this text are for your information and education only.

I make every attempt to speak authoritatively on the topics I discuss; however, nothing in this book is a replacement for the advice of a licensed professional.

Not only do laws change, but there are several legal subtleties beyond the scope of this book, best explained by a trusted CPA or legal advisor.

Many filmmakers already have a business set up for corporate production work they do on the side. Do you have a sole proprietorship, LLC, or other formal business structure? Good. That'll help you later. If you don't have a business registered yet, set one up before getting cash in hand.

I know it might *sound* scary, but it doesn't have to be.

Sole proprietorships should work for most low-budget filmmakers applying the FilmFuel method. It's the simplest form of business— inexpensive and crazy-easy to set up. However, suppose the budget you intend to raise is sizeable. In that case, you may need to register a Limited Liability Company (LLC) to protect personal assets and lend additional credibility to your production. Again, a financial or legal professional can help you evaluate these options based on your situation.

The bottom line? Before you get Fuelers, get a business license.

Alright. Enough housekeeping. Back to the fun stuff!

Premiere = Profit

Making money with FilmFuel rests on the idea of a legacy event (covered in detail in Part 6). For now, all you've gotta know is that this will be your official premiere with the film's cause taking center stage. It's a powerful way of building an audience and generating cash with your work. We used this model to launch *Orphaned Courage*, and it paid off handsomely.

When monetizing your premiere, you've got two options. The first is to donate all of the event's profits to charity.

If breaking even is a reasonable goal for your project, by all means, go this route. Donating all premiere profits to your chosen cause is the most fulfilling and direct way to make a meaningful difference with your film.

Unfortunately, this strategy has a critical downside. Because we are donating all profits, there's nothing left over for you or your future films. *Josiah, how is this sustainable? I've developed a bad habit—I like to eat!* Hold on, hold on! This is where the second option comes in.

You can make a sustainable difference without donating all your profits. How? By committing a *percentage* of your event's sales to charity instead.

This is the typical course of action I recommend to FilmFuel filmmakers to optimize your project for both impact and income. Before raising funds, simply select the percentage you're comfortable contributing. Perhaps 50% of everything that comes in (*proceeds*) or 50% of everything leftover (*profits*) is donated. Literally, this percentage you select could be anything. My recommendation is somewhere in the range of 10% to 50% of the event's profits, but there is room on both ends for additional generosity or diligent bootstrapping.

The key with either strategy is the vocabulary used when pitching.

In my case with *Orphaned Courage*, when I said, "The profits of this project are going to an adoption assistance fund," the key was saying *profits* instead of *proceeds*.

Profits, proceeds—same difference! Actually, the surest way to kill your event's profitability is to mix these up and commit proceeds instead of profits. Why?

"*Proceeds*" can mean every dollar made from the film, whereas "*profits*" means the dollars left after expenses are paid. Sizeable upfront expenses, such as a theater rental, are often necessary to guarantee a better turnout and create an event people will remember for years to come. The ability to offset those expenses with some ticket sales is a game-changer. By donating profits, you can cover these costs *and* make a difference with what remains.

Studios take this to an unethical extreme, often called "*Hollywood accounting,*" that creatively minimizes the on-paper profits of a project.

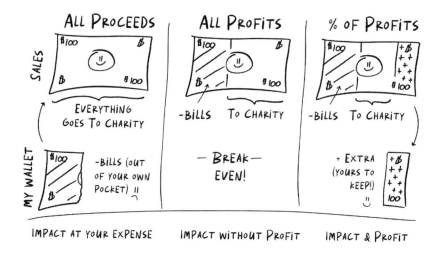

By inventing or inflating countless expenses, many studios can sidestep financial obligations to collaborators. Ever wonder why *Return of the Jedi,* with total box office earnings of $475 million, has—according to Lucasfilm—yet to make a profit? The film had a roughly 30-million-dollar budget. So, where did the rest of the money go?

Yeah. That's the half-billion-dollar question.

But there is a big difference between Hollywood's dubious financial practices and legitimately offsetting the cost of a theater rental for your premiere.

Don't overthink this. I have never had a Fueler interrogate me about my decision to commit the profits instead of the proceeds to charity. As long as your verbiage fully discloses your intentions on the front end, contributors know what they are getting themselves into and are free to decide what level of involvement they feel most comfortable with.

Donating a percentage of the pie instead of the whole thing is the right way to make a difference while remaining sustainable and ensuring you have the funds to keep making films. There's just one caveat. Please be clear from the onset about what is being given to charity. Commit to your desired percentage *before* approaching Fuelers. In this way, they can make a fully informed decision you can both feel good about.

8 | YOUR BATTLE BOOK

If you fall into any of the categories described in the previous chapters, you're in for a treat. Not only will I teach you to apply FilmFuel from pre-production to distribution, but I'll also give you tips and tricks from the trenches to help you fuel your current and future films.

In some corners of the military, officers are given *battle books*. These notebooks contain precious instructions that these soldiers refer to under fire. In life-or-death situations, they have everything they need to make it out alive. Think of this as your filmmaking battle book—at your side to save the day. This is the kind of book where you'll want to circle, underline, and scribble ideas in the margins. That's good. Dog-ear the heck out of it.

My recommendation? Read through it once to learn the process and absorb the ideas. Then, revisit the book as you start applying FilmFuel to your movie. Keep it handy as a reference as you walk through the steps in sequence. Additionally, use the *Take Action* portions of each section to personalize the training. Use the space to identify the best ways to apply the process directly to your project.

One quick footnote, I always enjoy hearing from FilmFuel filmmakers. Send your success stories to the email address in the back of the book (I read every one!), and you might just wind up in the second edition. Deal?

Where You're Headed

Before we conclude Part 1 of this book, let me give you a 30,000-foot preview of what to expect from the coming pages. We just explored the basics of FilmFuel film funding. From a high-level look at the process to some sustainable profitability hacks, I've already handed you several tools that will help you apply this framework later on.

Next up, I'll help you choose a cause and connect it deftly to the story of your film—arguably the most essential step in this entire process. Don't skim or skip it. This is something you need to get right. In Part 3, you'll create a list of future Fuelers. By the end, you'll be ready for the cold hard cash to make your movie. Part 4 gives you my script for approaching Fuelers and secret sauce tools for getting a "YES!" every time. I promise it'll be ten times easier than going it alone.

Part 5 explores other ways businesses can help you—things like providing food, locations, special vehicles, or even cast and crew. This is the most underutilized aspect of film funding. Don't believe me? Most of our filmmakers can cut their production budget in half after this.

Next, Part 6 dives deep into building a FilmFuel legacy event. Get ready to walk the red carpet as we establish venue options, generate press coverage, and create the kind of hype that sells out theaters.

Part 7 is your segue into the real world. With some final tools to help you put these strategies to use, you'll be ready to fuel your film.

There's a lot of ground to cover and value to discover. I hope you're as excited as I am. Let's end this section with one final thought. Who possesses the financial fuel that will help you make your movie? Is it your friends? Family? Some organization?

Think about it for a second.

It's actually businesses. (That's what you were gonna say, right? You're a smart cookie.) Businesses are the economic engines of the nation. In fact, according to the Small Business Association, they are responsible for two-thirds of all new jobs and 44% of the money generated by the United States. They have the financial means to lend a hand, and with the right cause and approach, you'll find them incredibly willing to help.

Ready to discover the cause that will ultimately fuel your film? Read on.

PART 2

FROM MOVIE TO MOVEMENT

9| CAUSE AND EFFECT

"ALRIGHT, BUDDY! WE'RE COMING TO PICK YOU UP! JUST A FEW MORE HOURS, AND YOU'LL BE OURS!"

I recently received a video from a couple about their newly adopted son. Why? For one simple reason. The charity *Orphaned Courage* supported had made this adoption possible. "*Look—we've already got the car seat! We can't wait to hold you in our arms!*" Tears were streaming down my face as I watched the precious scene unfold. As two parents embraced their new baby boy for the first time, all I could think was, "We were a part of this. My film was a part of this." I still can't believe that there are children out there somewhere who have a home of their own now *because* of my film. They're no longer orphans. *Because* of my film. There's something genuinely surreal about seeing people's lives transformed by the art we create. Because of *Orphaned Courage*, every 18 to 36 months in perpetuity, a new loving family will welcome another orphan child.

Just like that, a movie becomes a movement.

People out there desperately need your films to improve their circumstances. But unfortunately, most filmmakers never step into their calling and experience that level of impact. Most movies don't leave a legacy. Worse still, most are forgotten as soon as the credits roll. How sad is that?

Years of carefully writing, holding auditions, deciding on casting, managing logistics, raising funding, passionately filming, meticulously editing, and finally sharing only to—what? Be tossed aside? We all want to be remembered for our work. But *how* do you want to be remembered? As just another talented artist?

What about being remembered as someone who improved the world with their talents—a Serving Artist.

Everything else in this book is about you—funding *your* dreams, making *your* films, and building *your* career. Let's take a moment to consider the outward impact of using the FilmFuel method. Attaching a cause to your film might benefit you by multiplying your momentum, but it'll also irrevocably change the lives of others—the production team and viewer alike. It's ridiculously fulfilling. And once you get a taste for it, there's no going back.

Cause-driven filmmaking is nothing new.

If you step through the annals of history, media has often been the vessel used to shape culture. The 1988 film *The Thin Blue Line* drew the audience's attention to police corruption so heavily that it caused the conviction of a death row inmate to be overturned days before his execution. *Can anybody say "plot twist?"*

Films are so influential in directing the thoughts of society that Hitler used them as propaganda machines during the Second World War.

Stalin experienced it first-hand when he used the American film *The Grapes of Wrath* as a tirade against Western capitalism. The plan backfired. Instead of seeing capitalism lead to poverty, citizens in the USSR were drawn to the fact that even the poorest Americans had access to automobiles—an unattainable luxury for those in Soviet Russia. The point? Since the dawn of moving pictures, for better or worse, films have influenced culture.

There's a tremendous opportunity as filmmakers not just to tell a story, but to become architects of society, improving lives with our art.

FILMS SHIFT THE FUTURE.

10| AVOID FISCAL SPONSORSHIP

Before selecting a charity, we need to get one thing straight. FilmFuel is *not* Fiscal Sponsorship. Fiscal Sponsorship is the legal practice of a nonprofit organization "sponsoring" a project with its tax-exempt status. The project may then receive grants and funding otherwise only available to nonprofits. Although sponsorship is a viable route taken by filmmakers every day, the downsides are red tape and loss of control.

This approach is highly regulated because it involves an official agreement with a non-profit. As the project director, you must submit exhaustive reports on your use of funds. Although it does enable the supporting individuals and organizations to write their contributions off their taxes (quite appealing), it removes creative freedom from the filmmaking team.

For example, say your film (like *Orphaned Courage*) focuses on adoption, and you decide to connect with an adoption assistance fund using Fiscal Sponsorship. Your movie could extensively feature orphaned brothers and themes of adoption. But unless you mention the specific charity by name, the charity will potentially veto your sponsorship request because the connection between film and charity is too vague.* *But what about nuance and subtlety? I can't distract my viewers by naming specific charities throughout my movie!* Think *Truman Show* product placements, and I'm sure you'll understand my frustration.

Fiscal Sponsorship can be a terrific approach, but you must give up creative freedom to access the funding. Are you okay with your film turning into a public service announcement?

Yeah. I didn't think so.

However, if your film needs millions, you may want to give Fiscal Sponsorship a second chance. There are truckloads of grants and other opportunities for qualifying nonprofits and fiscally sponsored projects. Especially if you have a very specific cause you want to attach, or your film is *already* a documentary or public service announcement of sorts, this could be a valuable route to pursue.

FilmFuel, on the other hand, is uniquely indie-friendly. Although everything has red tape and legal considerations, FilmFuel helps minimize it. Bid *adieu* to the legal headaches of temporarily assuming a tax-exempt status or creating a nonprofit from scratch. *Too bad I can't offer tax write-offs for Fuelers, though! Sigh...* Not so fast! In Chapter 27, we'll explore how businesses can quasi-deduct their contribution to you *without* Fiscal Sponsorship and nonprofits. The result is similar, but the process is oh-so-simple.

---

* Although this is a legitimate gripe with Fiscal Sponsorship, it should be noted that some charities are willing to forgive some ambiguity as long as the film's values align with its mission. However, there are several drawbacks to consider, as the legalities are time-consuming and tedious. For a headache-free alternative, keep reading...

11| FINDING A MISSION

Finding the right mission for your movie is kind of like finding the right key to unlock a treasure chest. Until you hear that satisfying *click* when you give the right key a twist, the wealth inside can't help you. In the same way, the right cause will unlock your film's treasure trove of potential and help everything else fall into place—casting, funding, production, and distribution.

Get the cause right, and it's a cakewalk. *Click.*

Blindly choosing a cause and hoping it will work is like trying to open that strongbox with a butterknife. The key to properly open the chest isn't chosen at random, it's specifically designed to fit that lock. And without it, you won't get very far. Likewise, you must carefully select a cause related to your film. Not just related, but *deeply integrated* with your film's plot. Your success hinges upon it.

THE CAUSE MUST BE MOTIVATED BY THE STORY. ALWAYS.

The more deeply intertwined you get movie and mission, the more you stack the deck in your favor. Never tack on a random cause so you can mark it off your to-do list. Attaching an unrelated charity is the primary reason filmmakers fail to implement FilmFuel successfully.

CAUSE

Charity selection isn't something you want to *eeny meeny miny moe*. Take the time to get it right.

Okay, but how do you do that? The million-dollar question.

The most effective way is to *find a cause in your film's message*. Start with the film's plot. Then backtrack to find a moral premise* until you find the nail to hang a cause on. Let me take you through a real-life example and the progression of my thoughts as I discover a fitting charity. As we've discussed, *Orphaned Courage* is about two estranged orphan brothers uncovering their unexpected familial connection. At its core, the film is about identity—who you are is more than the family into which you're born.

To extract a cause from that moral message, I started working backward.

What *causes* speak to people's sense of belonging or help people struggling to find their identity? The film deals with a sad, negative reality—orphaned children. Well, is there an opposite from which I could extrapolate a cause? The "opposite" of orphaned children could be adoption. That's good. I've got several adopted cousins. There's a personal connection. What non-profit charities are associated with adoption? Orphanages?

Wait—adoptions are expensive, right? Are there charities that help families unable to afford adoptions? After a quick web search, I found my answer. They are called adoption assistance funds. The last step was simply finding a specific fund to work with. Boom. A cause deeply connected to my film's story—and my own.

Do you see how I started by pulling a thread? I took the moral premise and unraveled it until a cause became evident. The earlier you attach the charity to your story, the better and easier it will be for you. Much as the name "*Orphaned Courage*" already has the genesis of a cause woven in, tying the cause into your title, script, casting, and marketing will be easiest when you begin with the charity in mind. Because I attached our film to adoption early in the production process, we mentioned our purpose

---

* Although listing ideas for every possible theme is beyond the scope of this book, the Appendix also includes the five most common moral premises found in films and a few cause suggestions for each. If you are looking for examples or are struggling to identify your film's premise, consider giving that a look.

at every turn—including casting calls. It turns out the lead actor was passionate about the cause. It became the core reason he attached himself to the project. The earlier you connect the cause, the more effectively you will gather a passionate team around you.

If you're already writing your script or making your film—don't panic. I'll help you make it work. But if you have the option, start thinking of causes when your film is still in the idea stage.

Simply writing a robust moral premise into your script and giving thought to a few possible causes you could attach will set you up for success. You know the adage. The best time to plant a tree was twenty years ago, but the second-best time is today.

But what if I've finished pre-production? It could be that you've been handed a finished script and now need a healthy production budget. Or perhaps you're about to head into post-production and need funds for the final mile. Maybe you've already finished and just need help monetizing your film to fund the *next* one. You can still take advantage of the FilmFuel framework.

That's the good news.

However, if the story is set, you'll be digging a little deeper to extrapolate a cause from existing plot points and character arcs.

12| CASE STUDIES

Let's practice extracting a cause from a story by exploring a few examples across genres.* Suppose you have a film where the main character is a drug user or where addiction of some kind is a significant theme in your film. Your cause could be a specific rehabilitation program, clinic, or organization that assists such people.

If you're making a war movie, consider how your film's cause might be a nonprofit dedicated to military veterans, businesses owned by vets, or the treatment of post-traumatic stress disorder (PTSD). If your film involves a kidnapping, consider attaching a child safety or anti-human-trafficking organization.

If animals play a central role in your film, think about attaching an animal shelter. If your film takes place during hunting season, consider wildlife charities. Or, on the flip side, if your movie is *against* hunting, try some anti-hunting or endangered species charities.

Does your film involve underprivileged minorities? Consider causes that address those issues. If your movie deals with crime on the streets or the homeless, consider charities working to end homelessness. Try

---

* Consider this a quick reminder that there's a list of ideas for every film genre imaginable in the Appendix.

organizations supporting mental health if you're making a psychological thriller or a film that emphasizes someone at their breaking point.

If your film has an older cast or deals with parents and their children, consider charities that support senior citizens or family development. Whether your film is a gory horror film or deals with someone needing an organ transplant, heart associations would also be a cause worth attaching. You heard that right. You can use a horror film to make a difference. There are many ways to be creative, even clever or ironic, when tying the cause to your story.

If there's a motivated death in the story—for example, a father's death that motivates a son through the rest of the film, you could extract a cause from that. There are two ways to approach this. Your first option would be to find a cause that aligns with the cause of death (ex. leukemia) or circumstances of death (ex. drunk-driving car accident) already existing in the script. Alternatively, you could write the sickness or incident into your story and donate to the charities finding a cure. This option won't fit everyone, but it could be worth considering.

13| MORE TIPS, JUST 'CAUSE

What if I'm making a sci-fi or fantasy film? What cause would a James Bond movie fit? I get it. Some films are more challenging to find specific purposes for than others. Here are a few pointers that might make this process a little easier. If the cause isn't as apparent, focus on the human element in the film. No matter what galaxy your movie transports us to, certain aspects will make the story and characters relatable to *our* world. The film could take place on Mars, and you're going to have dialogue or plot points relatable to earthlings, right?

Work to tie in *those* elements. Take the movie *Interstellar* as an example.

Beyond the obvious space-exploration nonprofits related to the story, you could also focus on the movie's humanity. The moral premise is the preciousness of time, and the Make-A-Wish Foundation would be an excellent fit. Find relatable, human beats and story threads to build a cause around.

Niche or Broad?

When choosing a cause to connect, be careful not to drill down too far. You don't want to select a charity so niche that only a few people are passionate about it. Although you also don't want a cause so broad and generic that the film's purpose loses relevance, I would always err on the side of expansive reach. Why? More people affected by the cause equals more people interested in your film. The more people interested in your film, the easier funding will be. What's the punchline? The more *connected* to the story and the more *universal* the impact, the more people will get behind the cause, film, distribution, and premiere.

If you're still having trouble nailing down a cause, think locally.

You will likely approach local businesses for funding soon, so consider what causes they care about. Many don't realize that companies are eager to demonstrate their humanity. They're not as cold, sleek, and impersonal as people make them out to be. Instead, they want to show they care about and give back to their local communities. Need proof? Check out your area baseball team and see how many local businesses have their logos plastered on the jerseys and stands! These businesses are often aware of their social responsibility and routinely search for opportunities to give back to their community.

You can leverage this by finding a *local cause* to link to your film. Since *Orphaned Courage* was filmed in Kentucky, I focused on a charity that could assist Kentucky families wanting to adopt. Having a local connection makes getting airtime on local media more accessible and motivates the community to support your project in unexpected ways.

Combining the last two tips by finding a cause that affects many people *and* has a local component can be a particularly compelling strategy. For example, a few years ago, in our sleepy town in the southeast, a police officer was killed on patrol. At the time, many fundraisers, marathons, and events supported the officer's family and *other victims of cop shootings*. Because of the local connection, there was a big push for bumper stickers on every car and blue porch lights on every house in support of local law enforcement. The entire community rallied together in support of this cause.

Another example of a local connection would be in the event of a regional natural disaster—snow, flood, fire, or storm—where your project joins the relief efforts. Look at your local news and get creative. Every other week there's a crisis you could play a part in ending!

Score Bankable Talent

Want to leverage a cause to get A-list talent for your film? Consider researching those I lovingly call *Actorvists*—actors passionate about social causes. For example, actor Danny Trejo is known for his philanthropic efforts with at-risk youth, Jim Caviezel and Brad Pitt are passionate about adoption, and Scarlett Johansson is dedicated to ending poverty in third-world countries. To find out what your desired actor cares about, search their name and "charity work" or look into places they have held speaking engagements.

If you come up empty, try scouring Wikipedia for their personal stories or motivations and find causes related to those. Many talented actors have risen from broken circumstances and are passionate about helping others in similar situations. When you reach out (either through the related charity you choose or directly), strongly emphasize the cause to the talent or their agent.

If you have a "kinda" connection to a big-name actor through friends or colleagues, this would also be an excellent way to make that first move. Find a cause they're passionate about, connect it to your film (or heck, write a movie around it!), and get them involved. If you strike out on A-list, try the same approach with B- or C-list actors. Someone with star power will be passionate about the same values and open to collaborating on a meaningful project.

ACTORVIST

(NOUN) A PHILANTHROPIC CELEBRITY WHO ALREADY USES THEIR INFLUENCE FOR IMPACT.

14| CHOOSING CHARITIES

Once you have a few ideas for causes (perhaps adoption, suicide prevention, or treating leukemia), it's time to pick a specific charity to partner with. To make this process easier, I created the *FilmFuel Assessment*—an interactive tool that makes custom charity recommendations based on the unique content of your film.

Now, don't expect an exhaustive list. My goal with this assessment is to give you a starting point that saves you from the frustration of a blank page and countless hours of effort. I've cataloged 200 charities into more than 40 unique film genres (from *comedy* to *horror* and everything in between) to kickstart your charity selection and idea generation. There's nothing else like this out there. Best of all, it's free for anyone with a copy of the FilmFuel book—my gift to you with no strings attached. Take the assessment at **www.josiahstendel.com/filmfuelextras**.

To be clear, the recommendations in this assessment are based on cursory internet sleuthing. I do not have relationships with these charities, nor can I endorse them. As with anything, please do your due diligence before connecting with a charity.

If you decide to choose an organization the tool recommends, get in touch with the charity first. See where money is going and if that fits your project's vision.

Web Search

In addition to the *FilmFuel Assessment* on the book extras website, other ways to find charities include doing a web search for the cause (such as "veterans" or "homelessness") and adding the word "charities," "non-profits," or "organizations" to the end of it. Search a few websites and note any organization with a *donate* button or a disclosure that they are a 501(c)(3) non-profit organization.

Those would all be potential matches.

Community

Next, you could source charities from the local community. Churches and ministries (non-profits themselves) regularly interact with various local-impact organizations. Asking churches for introductions could save you some time finding and vetting potential charities.

Look at who sponsors the 5K races and marathons in your area or which causes they raise money to support. Make a few calls to find the destination of the event's proceeds. Exploring existing partnerships between projects and donors is a practical way to generate reputable charity ideas.

15| THE FOURTH WALL

If you're struggling to link a cause or none of the others seem to click for you, there is one final option you could explore as a FilmFuel hail-Mary—a *Fourth Wall Cause*.

In theater, the fourth wall is the imaginary divide between the stage and the audience. When watching a movie, the fourth wall is the television screen. It's what separates you from what you see on-screen.

Theater actors will sometimes intentionally *break the fourth wall*. They'll run through the audience or address them directly—dissolving the illusion that the performance is reality and drawing the audience's attention to the fact that it is all just a show.

Although a little meta, a *Fourth Wall Cause* is focused on filmmaking itself. You're drawing attention to the fact that this is a film. If no other charity fits, you could attach a cause related to filmmaking as an art. For example, it could be a promotion of

local, regional, national, or even international entertainment and arts. Your film could raise awareness for teen filmmakers, woman filmmakers, disabled artists, or even local film incentives. Essentially, a Fourth Wall Cause brings attention to the making of the film, the people behind it, or a cause directly related to the arts and entertainment industry.

My Fourth Wall Film

When I made *The Cold Season* in 2019, I decided that a Fourth Wall was the way to go. The film itself wasn't depressing, but the characters discussed the ethics of euthanasia (not something I endorse, of course) and asked some tough questions about the preciousness of life without offering many answers. Because of the film's fatalistic nature, I thought it best not to attach a charity and instead go meta to support the film industry. My cause became demonstrating to other low-budget filmmakers how to make a meaningful film on a shoestring budget. Did it work? I documented the 50-day process of creating the film—from casting to distribution—and amassed a following of nearly 15,000 fans on social media. The film itself got many rave reviews from critics and won dozens of awards at festivals across the globe, even making it into the Academy-Award qualifying Nashville Film Festival as an official selection.

16| HOW TO DECIDE

At this point, you might be feeling some information overload. If so, that's okay. It's by design. For any film you decide to make, I want you to have examples, options, and ideas to refer back to. But if you're like most FilmFuel filmmakers, you've now probably got more options than you know what to do with. I don't want to see you drown in opportunity. Ultimately, making any decision is better than wasting time caught in indecision.

ONE DECISIVE ACTION IS WORTH A THOUSAND GOOD IDEAS.

But how do I know which one to choose?

Here's my advice to you. Where do you feel life? When filmmakers go through this process, most recall a pivotal *ah-ha* moment where they immediately identified their film's cause. Don, one of my OG FilmFuel filmmakers, recalls, "The moment FilmFuel was explained, I got a ton of ideas. From there, I was able to narrow down my film's cause within a few minutes."

Include Your Past

As you evaluate your options, think about charity selection as a Venn diagram. You're looking for the overlap between something story-motivated,

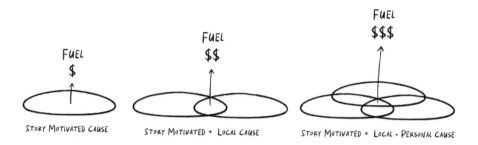

local, and personal to you. Most important is the connection to your story, but a close second is a personal connection to your own story.

Raising money for underprivileged or underrepresented people is impressive. But you want to answer *why* it means something to you. You're a filmmaker. You get the power of story, right? This is *your* story. It's the missing piece that transforms admirers into supporters. People won't care if they can't understand *why you care*. Your narrative should help people personally identify with your cause and your motivation for making the film. Combining your movie, a related charity, and a personal experience is a powerful trifecta that we will leverage to build a tribe around your project.*

Does any cause stand out as something you or a close friend experienced? Are any causes on your list ones you're personally passionate about? For example, the *Orphaned Courage* cause of adoption was near to my heart because I have four adopted cousins. My experience inspired the film's cause. Look for the personal connection that gets an *"Aww!"* when you tell someone else about it.

As you were going through the descriptions above, the *FilmFuel Assessment*, or a web search—what sparked excitement? What made you go, *"Ooh, that'd be cool."* Go with that gut-impulse connection to your film's message and your personal story. If it stirs up emotion in you, imagine what it will do for others!

---

* A personal connection is so critical to FilmFuel success, that for your next film, consider *starting* with a cause deeply intwined with your past and *then* crafting a compelling narrative around it.

If you can't find a cause related to your film, you're dead in the water. Go back, take the *FilmFuel Assessment*, and keep brainstorming. I promise you, there's a cause out there for your film.

On the other hand, if you can't find a personal connection to any of the causes, don't panic. Try turning the mirror on your team. Is there a cause deeply related to the past of a key production partner? If not, find a powerful story of

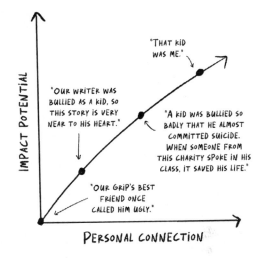

someone *else* your chosen charity has impacted. Charities will often publish these anecdotes as testimonials. But beware—in either of these two scenarios, the story must be *crazy strong*. Pro tip: Own the narrative. Personalize it by sharing not only how the charity affected that person but also how *their* story affected *you*. However you choose to do it, align your film's mission with your own backstory for faster funding and deeper influence.

Include Your Team

Once you have your cause, announce the new social mission to your cast and crew. Better yet, involve your team in the cause brainstorming-and-selection process. Stephen, another FilmFuel filmmaker, discovered how valuable crew participation could be. After an enthusiastic pre-production meeting, he told me, "I pitched the framework to the crew, and they loved it! They all drew up ideas of charities they wanted to support through the show. Everybody got excited by the idea. Ultimately, we went with the cause our two writers chose. They both wish there were more opportunities for children from poorer households." Involving your team in selecting the film's purpose will deepen their commitment to your project.

My film becomes *our* film.

17 | I GOT A CAUSE! WHAT NOW?

Congrats! You picked a charity. That's the most critical step of this entire process. You've officially moved from Starving Artist to Serving Artist.

Give yourself a high-five. Or clap, I guess. Whatever.

What's next? First, reach out to the charity and tell them about your project. It isn't a prerequisite, and some FilmFuel filmmakers have found non-profits to be rather uncommunicative. In that case, you can always cut them a check like any other donor would, through their website or by mail. However, if you try to get them involved, there are many potential benefits.

Your outreach doesn't need to be fancy. Just say, "I'm making a short film about [...]" and insert your film's logline. Follow that up with "to raise money and awareness for [your cause]," describing the people they serve with their charity. End with the personal connection and explain why you're reaching out. Here's how I would say it:

"Hi. My name is Josiah Stendel, and later this year, I'm making a film about two estranged orphan brothers who grew up in entirely different homes and their incredible journey to reunite. I want to make this film to raise money and awareness for orphaned children in my state of Kentucky.

Because I have four adopted cousins, the cause of adoption is near to my heart. I'm reaching out because I'd like my project to support the work you guys do in this area, and I wanted to know more about you and the way you serve."

This simple message starts to build a relationship with the organization. Your first goal is simply a response. Get them excited about your project.

Some FilmFuel filmmakers lose steam when they excitedly send their emails to their desired charities but don't hear anything in response. Keep in mind that smaller non-profits (and even some larger ones) still live in the dark ages. They may not have a designated person monitoring their email. Even if they do, they may simply miss your message.

You can try a follow-up email if you haven't heard back in the first five days, but it may be more effective to get them on the phone with the same simple objective of making contact. Since most non-profits regularly take calls as a source of donations, they will undoubtedly pick up the phone or return your voicemail.

So you received a sign of life! Great.

Ask them if they'd be willing to share a list of their corporate sponsors with you—those businesses and organizations (*not* individuals) who regularly contribute to them. Don't be surprised if you run into policies that keep them from sharing that information with you. Many charities highly prioritize the privacy of their donors. The charity we chose, for example, wasn't comfortable disclosing this. But if they are willing, it would be a goldmine for you. Imagine being handed a list of businesses already opening their wallets to support this cause! The fundraising portion of the FilmFuel process would be a walk in the park.

So, be sure to try—maybe you'll strike gold.*

We'll discuss this in detail in Part 3, but if the charity *does* send you a list, you can then reach out to those organizations (making sure to mention

---

* Some donors give under the condition of anonymity, but many—specifically corporations—don't mind the recognition (it makes them look good!). If you can't get a master list from the charity, consider checking out the non-profit's newsletter, blog, or annual report for major donors that they have publicly thanked.

the connection your film has to the charity) and that the charity sent you their way. This approach is a great way to break the ice with a new potential Fueler who is already involved with the same cause.

When you start promoting your film, you can reach out to the charity again to have them share your project on their social media channels. To set yourself up for a "yes," approach them with a pre-written post that they can seamlessly copy and paste onto their social media pages—don't forget a graphic and link—to promote your project and the connection to their charity. Your ask might be as simple as this: "Could you copy and paste this to your social media to spread awareness and build interest for this film?"

More often than not, they'll be willing to help you out. It benefits them too, right?

Now that we've laid a solid foundation, let's dive deep into film funding. In Part 3, I'll show you the secret-sauce approach—what to say to businesses to get your budget fully funded. Before you turn this page, though, you need to choose your FilmFuel monetization model. Are you going to donate all of your legacy premiere profits* to charity? A percentage? What fits the vision of your film best?

We've learned a lot together in these last few chapters—unearthing the cause hidden in your film's story and then bridging the gap to a specific charity. You gave your film a purpose and chose a specific recipient for your film's impact. Couldn't be more proud.

My friend, you are now ready to fund your film.

---

* Do you remember why we say *profits* and not *proceeds*? Proceeds includes every single dollar that comes in, while profits are the proceeds less any expenses.

» TAKE ACTION » » » » » » » »

Brainstorming time. Meet with your team and divide a blank sheet of paper into four columns.* Start listing the moral *themes* of your film in the first column. What are you trying to teach people? What's the lesson?

Next, take each theme and spend a few minutes discussing them in turn. What causes could each theme be connected to? Add these related *causes* into the second column.

Then, take one cause at a time and research related *charities* that your film could support. You could use the *FilmFuel Assessment* on the book extras website, browse the internet, or check out local sources. Add any specific charities of interest to the third column for consideration.

Finally, go down the list and brainstorm any possible *personal connections* you or your team has to any of the themes, causes, or charities. Add these to the final column.

Decide on a charity. Evaluate your options based on the criteria in Chapter 16, and choose the best fit for your project. Reach out to this charity of choice and get them excited about your project. If they are willing, have them send you a list of their corporate donors.

Finally, commit to a FilmFuel monetization model. If your film is entirely for a social cause, allocate all profits to charity. If you want to make a sustainable career from this approach, select a percentage of profits to commit.

* Alternatively, visit the book extras page at www.josiahstendel.com/filmfuelextras to download a printable worksheet version of this four-column exercise.

PART 3

GOT FUEL?

18| TARGET ACQUIRED

TEEN DIRECTED MOVIE AFTER GETTING BRACES OFF—
AND GOT HIS ORTHODONTIST TO INVEST.

I'm not even joking. That was the headline. It still makes me cringe. Which sixteen-year-old wants to make the front page with *that* written about him? Oh well. Mistakes were made. No such thing as bad publicity, right? The point of reliving this embarrassment is that I got local businesses to contribute to my project (even at a young age)—and you can too. I promise, funding your film doesn't have to be intimidating. It can even be fun! If it happens to be a little uncomfortable at times (like my front-page debut), it'll all be worthwhile if your dreams are funded and lives are changed.

Still got that blank check you filled out after reading the first chapter? Good. Let's make it rain.

Finding Fuelers

Although possible, it is unlikely that a *single* business will be able to fund you fully. Instead, piece together the funding from several Fuelers. Your goal is a portfolio of smaller commitments that equal your desired film budget. Before we approach anyone, however, let's identify the target.

The best Fuelers align with the plot of your film—for example, a theme park for an action flick, a gun range for a war film, or an escape room for a thriller. The alignment between topic and business will open up doors for you. More on this in Part 7.

But what other kinds of businesses make good Fuelers, and where can you find them?

Horse racing is a big deal on my side of the country. For context, the Kentucky Derby typically brings in north of $400 million in a single weekend. However, here's something few people know. Most of those standing with the champion in the Winner's Circle simply wrote a check to be there. They don't breed, train, or even ride horses.

Then why care? Why pay to be there?

Racing is a flashy industry, much like filmmaking.

Funding films or racehorses involves identifying those who will likely never be directly involved in the industry but whose checkbook gives them access to the action. Fuelers will fund your film for several reasons—more on this later—but the core reason for contributing is emotional. They want prestige. Status. Something cool to brag about at the country club.

They desire the respect of standing in the Winner's Circle.

THE WINNER'S CIRCLE

Where can you find these well-to-do winners? The most obvious place is your charity's Rolodex of corporate donors. If you can get your hands on a list like this, funding your film will be a cakewalk. Go down the list, approach each business, and pitch them your film with the techniques you will learn in the next few chapters. These Fuelers are the lowest-hanging fruit imaginable.

Harvest their support first.

If you can't get a list of donors from your charity (like most filmmakers I've consulted), don't worry. There are two other sources of FilmFuel. First, funding can come from any business with a **personal connection** to you. These are places you frequent or business owners you know.

Secondly, you can generate FilmFuel from **network connections**. Friends of friends. These may be business owners your buddies know, for example. These two groups are your gateway to a fully-funded film. Did you feel that? Chills. It's getting real.

19| DO I KNOW YOU?

Start by making a list of business owners you know. Maybe a former colleague left his job to start his own company. Or perhaps a family member owns a small business. Organize your list with those most likely to help you at the top—they're also low-hanging fruit. Why? You have the most personal credibility and rapport with these Fuelers.

Or perhaps you don't know any business owners, but at the top of your list is that coffee shop you've gone to every morning for ten years. You know the one. Where you thought, *"Man, I'm here so often, I need to take out stock in this place."* Maybe you've talked to the manager once before and have at least a little relational currency with them. That's great too. If you're a *young'un* like I was, maybe it's a business your family has frequented for years or one owned by a family friend. Put your best contacts at the top of the list.

Ahh, I'm drawing a blank, Josiah. Well, something else you can try is walking through your list of friends or followers on your favorite social media platform. Check out where your contacts are employed. Maybe you'll notice a friend from college is now a manager at such-and-such place.

Add her to the list.

Perhaps you're reminded of a friend with influence.

Add 'em too.

Think too about recent errands you've run. Maybe you visit a particular dry cleaner, supermarket, or restaurant regularly. Think about any locales you've recently purchased from or places you like to eat. If they know you or you know them, put 'em on the list.

Let me give you a few more rapid-fire ideas to get your creative juices flowing. Local insurance agents, dentists, orthodontists, and doctors.

Don't forget, my orthodontist was the first to cut me a check for my film.* I'll always be grateful. People-oriented professional service businesses care about their image and often have the resources to invest in marketing. Most people have a personal connection to one of these places. If you don't, poll your cast and crew about who their doctor or dentist is.

Lawyers, accountants, and financial advisors are also constantly building relationships with small businesses. If you have a long-standing relationship with a legal or tax professional, they are not only potential sources of funding but also excellent sources of other Fuelers.

Did you recently buy a car or home? Dealerships and real estate agents can also be goldmines. Buying and selling high-ticket items like houses and cars makes for a competitive, cash-rich business. They, too, will be looking for new ways of getting their name out there in the community.

All these are personal connections you can leverage into a list of potential contributors. Keep in mind that spontaneous opportunities will arise. You never know when you'll run into someone who can help. When we approached a local coffeehouse, for example, and pitched our project to management, the employees who overheard were so moved that they started volunteering gifts from their own pockets.

"We get a free pound of coffee a month as a job perk," one explained. "Could you give mine to someone on the cast or crew as a thank-you for what you're doing?"

Another piped up, "Here, have my bag of coffee too!"

---

* While writing this section, I learned dentists have generously (even indiscriminately to their own peril) been funding films since the 1950s. Some industry insiders scoff and call this old saw, but it's how I got "first money in" for my movie. If it worked for me, it just might work for you too.

DO I KNOW YOU?

Before long, each staff member had sacrificed their personal product allowance to support our project. Yes, we received financial support from the business as well, but what really surprised and impressed me was the generosity of the workers. We had enough gifts for each of our team members to feel valued and seen. And that was priceless.

The moral here is don't be surprised if most of your resources ultimately come from unexpected places. As you go about your day, look for and lean into those serendipitous moments.

20| A FRIEND OF YOURS IS A FRIEND OF MY FILM

There's a mantra in the world of business that says your financial performance is best estimated by looking at your connections. In other words, your network is your net worth. Why? The value lies in the *access* your network provides. It's not selfish. It's a math problem. The more people you are connected to, the more potential for resources to be exchanged.

Not only do these connections offer possible sources of financing, but an inner circle of expert mentors is the way to overcome any challenge you might face—personally and professionally. Having a vast arsenal of resources at your fingertips is key to success.

$$\left(?\right) + \left(?\right) + \left(?\right) + \left(\smile\right) + \left(?\right) + \left(?\right) + \left(?\right) = \$\$\$$$

Nowhere is this as valid as in film funding.

Step one, involve your cast and crew. Find out what businesses they have personal connections to. Next, tell your friends about your project. *You're not asking them for money.* I repeat—don't beg your buddies for cash. Instead, ask these friends to connect you with potential supporters. Because of the cause, expect a warm reception. People are more willing to hear and help you out when you've got an outward-facing purpose for your project.

The goal is to ask friends for referrals to Fuelers (owners or managers) in their circles who might want to support your project. I guarantee you have friends with unique direct connections to local Fuelers, but you'll never find them if you don't ask around.

After exploring these options, you should have a solid list of businesses that you could approach right now. Whoa there, grasshopper. I didn't mean *right now,* right now. Finish this section first. We'll figure out exactly what to say in your pitch to maximize your chances of a loud and resounding *"YES!"*

One final note here, don't be afraid of approaching businesses cold turkey.

Although the biggest checks I've received for films have come from organizations that knew me, some of my funding came from businesses I approached without any connection. It *is* possible. I still recommend starting where you have an existing relationship or a referral from a friend to make it easier, but don't let that stop you from reaching higher.

Honestly, an approach I've always wanted to try is visiting local sports fields and writing down all the sponsor logos I see. Why? Most of these are small businesses that are already giving money to enhance their image in the local community. Those businesses are already aware of social engagement and care about their reputation.

They would be an excellent fit for the FilmFuel model.

Going somewhere you're invited or known is best, but armed with the strategies in the following chapters, you can walk into any local establishment and still have a great chance of walking out with a check.

21| THE "P" WORD

In my experience, the process of pitching often feels intimidating. Could it be because there's confusion about what to say and how? Or maybe you don't feel like a confident extrovert? Whatever the reason, as soon as filmmakers hear the word "pitch" for the first time, their pulse invariably quickens, and they start freaking out.

"I'M NOT SO GREAT IN FRONT OF PEOPLE. DO I CALL THEM? DO I EMAIL THEM? DO I GO IN PERSON? WHAT SHOULD I DO, JOSIAH? WHEN? WHERE? HOW?!"

It's okay.

We'll take this one step at a time. It's not that scary, I promise. Believe it or not, you're already an experienced pitcher.

Convincing an actor to join your cast? That's pitching.

Asking someone out? That's pitching, too.

Keeping your cat off your laptop during a team call? That's—well, that's not pitching. That's impossible. The point is that *every time you make a request, present an idea, or want your way, it's a pitch.*[*] Without realizing it, you're already making dozens of pitches a day.

The only difference is now you'll get paid for it.

---

[*] In fact, I'm pitching you on pitching right now!

The following sections will lay the groundwork for approaching businesses with practical tools and actionable advice to set you up for a successful pitch. In Chapter 29, you'll master the Quick Pitch formula I used to get over $75,000 in resources for my short film. And by the end of the section, crafting your pitch will be a matter of filling in the blanks.

22| EMAIL, CALL, OR FACE-TO-FACE

Believe it or not, my highest-value pitch was done not in person or via the phone—but by email.

Here's how it went down. I emailed the company's founder, and she mailed me back a check. Boom. That was it. Because these Fuelers already knew me, there was no in-person interaction needed. Wouldn't it be nice if all it took to get your film funded was sending a few emails? Of course, it's not always that easy, but sometimes it is.

If you want to see the exact email I sent out to potential Fuelers I knew,* check out **www.josiahstendel.com/filmfuelextras**. It was likely the most profitable single email I have ever sent. In addition to the example message, you will find a downloadable template version where you can fill in your

---

* A quick word of warning here. You will notice the email I sent was relatively long. Because I knew the people I sent this to, I was confident they would read the whole thing. And it worked! However, if your message is more of a "first date" (read: you aren't as familiar with this person), I would highly recommend keeping your first touch brief to maximize your chances of hearing back from them.

cause, logline, movie title, and more to craft your pitch and start reaching out to familiar Fuelers right away.

How do you know when to email, call, or go in person? It all depends on your proximity to the Fueler. Here's my rule of thumb. If the connection is already warm and receptive to you, familiar with your enthusiasm, and falls into the "very likely to help" category, you're probably fine to email or call.

However, whenever possible, go in person for this simple reason: *passion is more contagious in person.*

IT'S SIMPLE. DON'T MISS THIS. PASSION SELLS.

To fund your film, your priority must be *passion transfer—your* passion needs to become *their* passion.

When you pitch a Fueler—whether over email or over dinner—they will mirror the level of enthusiasm they perceive in you. What you want is that they become as enthusiastic about your film as you are. That's when funding becomes effortless.

Isn't it harder to turn someone down when they ask you for something in person?

The same applies here.

When you're not face-to-face, the person you're pitching isn't able to hear your intonation. The communication comes across as cold and impersonal. That's no good. The single best way to ensure passion transfer is to be in the same room with them.

Although I have found virtual pitches to be slightly less effective overall, in situations where face-to-face is not possible, video

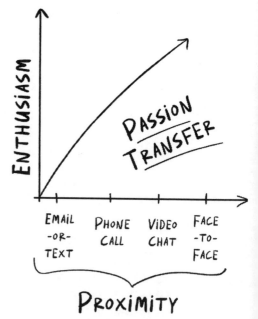

conferencing is a fantastic alternative. Not to mention, it suddenly opens up opportunities beyond your immediate geography. As we keep going, keep in mind that all the same in-person pitching tips and tricks apply when pitching via Zoom.

23|
PREPARING FOR THE PITCH

I was fifteen years old when I won my first settlement case. That's not a typo. Yours truly went toe-to-toe negotiating a copyright dispute with a billion-dollar organization before I was even old enough to drive.

Not necessarily a resume builder but talk about David facing down Goliath!

Earlier that year, I had worked closely with a representative from this organization (let's call him Joe), producing a commercial for free with the understanding that I would use the finished project as an example of my work. I was still getting my start and was humbled by the opportunity. What could go wrong?

In a dramatic process that started three days after production and dragged on for nine months afterward, the organization disavowed my rights to the footage. They suddenly stated that *they* owned it and that my "claim of ownership" came as a "complete shock." Finally, the organization called a summit to resolve this. Invitations were extended to me, Joe, his team, and the organization's legal counsel.

My mom went along as my moral support—and chauffeur. Walking into the meeting, I remember her expressing concerns, "Josiah, don't let them take advantage of you."

After we sat down and exchanged pleasantries, the organization's attorney, a stout, balding man in his mid-fifties, leaned across the table. He asked me for my side of the story with a strong southern drawl, "What's this all about then?"

I briefly explained.

"Now that's a problem, Josiah. You don't own the copyright to the footage," he interrupted condescendingly. "It's called a Work for Hire. The company that hires you owns the copyright. Not you."

I sat there for a second.

"But is it a Work for Hire if I didn't get paid?"

At that, the attorney's eyes got wide. He spun around.

"He didn't get paid?"

Joe swallowed hard. "N-No, sir, he offered to do it for free, but we didn't know—" "Where's the contract?" No response. The attorney slammed his fist on the mahogany conference table with a shout. "C'mon, tell me you've got a contract!" Only stony silence answered his glare. "We're gonna talk later," he hissed at Joe, "I've warned you about this."

Although Joe was in the hot seat, I learned the importance of contracts (even for volunteer projects) that day.

He turned back to me, his tone suddenly different—softer, but still just as patronizing.

"So, what do you really have here? It's not footage, is it? I mean, what is footage *really*?"

He looked towards the ceiling, searching.

"It's—it's electrons! On a hard drive!" He gave a little laugh.

"*You're* electrons!" I retorted. Well, not really. But I sure wanted to. I didn't bite, instead just looking at him incredulously—not sure what to say. He continued, unfazed, "You're trying to tell me that you *own* these electrons?"

"My footage—," I finally responded.

"Ah! Your electrons!" He corrected me, almost comically wagging his sausage-like finger in my face.

"We both know it's my intellectual property."

With a theatrical sigh, my Goliath sat back in his chair and crossed his arms. "Alright, Perry Mason—how do you propose we solve this?"

With carefully measured words, I stated my terms.

The attorney's ears perked up. He called for a huddle and spoke with Joe and his team—clearly advising them to take the deal. I felt a kick under the table. "Are you sure you know what you're doing?" my mom whispered, panicky. I assured her I did.

It was a win-win, and the attorney knew it. He couldn't shake my hand quickly enough.

A few days later, I got a letter titled *Stendel Settlement & Release Agreement*.

Oddly enough, the story doesn't end there. For several years, this organization became one of Made You Look Media's biggest accounts. Standing my ground, facing down this giant, led to one of our most profitable clients in the last decade. Why am I sharing this? Had I not come prepared with a proposed resolution or a defense against his stupid Work for Hire argument, I might have lost the rights to my "electrons."

In the same way, when you pitch your film, come prepared with tangible pitch files to show you mean business. *Wait—pitch files?* Don't worry. After I give an overview of everything you need, I'll share how you can download fill-in-the-blank versions of each and customize 'em for your project. They're amazing. I genuinely wish that I had access to these when I started.

Ready to discover the tools you'll need for your pitch?

24| ONE-SHEET

The **One-Sheet** is essentially your film's resume.

It is all the information a potential Fueler might need: what your film is about, how much money you need, what the money is paying for, and how the Fueler will be getting a return (in other words, your distribution plan). This One-Sheet includes a general budget breakdown that delineates how much is allotted for cast and crew, catering, equipment, and locations.

Although from the name you might assume it should be a single page, exact length is unimportant as long as you provide a concise collection of decision-critical information. Because your Fuelers are not investors and your One-Sheet is not a prospectus, your plans can be broad and hedged by reality. I hope you just breathed a sigh of relief. You don't need a business plan to secure film funding. You just need enough detail to paint a picture of your film's future. The brass tacks.

On previous projects, I typically stated the end-goal was distribution through on-demand streaming services. I then qualified my promises by saying "services *like* Amazon and Netflix" since I wasn't sure if it would be possible to get onto one of the major streaming platforms—spoiler alert, we did!

If you'd like to see a no-frills One-Sheet example and a print-ready template, visit the book extras page at **www.josiahstendel.com/filmfuelextras**. By using this blueprint, you will save so much time creating your own One-

Sheet. If you want to go the extra mile, add some eye-catching visuals to sell your story. They always speak louder than words.

How do you use the One-Sheet in your approach? Think of it as the longer printed version of your pitch for those who want more information.

Because you don't want to take up too much time, you want to keep your actual pitch short and punchy—let them signal interest or disinterest quickly—and save the One-Sheet for those who want to learn more before pulling out their checkbook.

If you were to walk into a business and start going through every minute detail of the project and the cause, the Fueler would begin to fatigue. At that point, every second that goes by decreases your chances of walking out of there with a check. You have to lead them to a quick decision.

Think about the time you bought your phone. Whether you consciously realize it or not, you were first drawn to a particular brand or model because of how it made you feel. Perhaps it was the phone's sleek design, the cutting-edge features, or the brand's status and reputation.

Once you made the purchase, however, you used logical reasoning to justify your decision. For example, if someone asked you why you bought it, you likely cited the phone's processing speed, battery life, camera quality, or other objective features that aligned with your needs.

The emotional appeal of the phone's design or brand reputation initially captured your attention and motivated your choice to buy, while the logical reasons made you feel more confident in your decision and helped you justify it to yourself and others. This is known as the *Emotional Reasoning Theory*.

People Don't Buy Because of Logic.

They need an emotional reason to commit first (in your case, the cause) and then some logical evidence to back up their decision (the One-Sheet) and bolster their confidence.

Guide a Fueler to a quick yes based on the positive emotions of being a part of something meaningful, and then affirm their decision. Help them understand the benefit to their business with the One-Sheet and other materials so they feel good about their choice. Make sense?

25| PROOF OF CONCEPT

A picture is worth a thousand words. A moving picture is worth—well, a whole lot more. How much exactly? It has been estimated that one minute of video is as persuasive as approximately 1.8 million words. That's the equivalent of yakking for over a hundred hours! Using video in your pitch will drastically increase your chances of securing FilmFuel.

Especially if you're a young filmmaker or don't have as much previous work to show, producing a simple proof of concept (POC) trailer or short film before walking into your first pitch would be wise.

A trailer is typically plenty for your pitch. But, if you're producing a full-length feature film and want to go all out, a short film can do wonders. I had the privilege of DP'ing a concept short for a Hollywood actor and dear friend of mine, Silvio Wolf Busch. My friend pitched this particular project to industry executives with the hopes of developing the feature. The shoot involved a cast and crew of hundreds and the largest assembly of functional World War II weaponry since May of 1945. Nothing small or easy about it.

Although the result was breathtaking, not every proof of concept needs sixteen tanks. In fact, let me caution you—don't get so hung up on the proof of concept that it stalls the effort to produce your actual film. Rather a simple one-minute, one-scene teaser that gets finished quickly than a massive production that keeps you from ever moving forward with the real feature. Keep your eye on the prize.

Yes, any concept trailer will involve some time investment, but having something visual to show Fuelers is powerful. It's an opportunity for you to show off your chops as a filmmaker and get them jazzed up with a sneak preview.

Again, it doesn't need to be fancy. You won't be showing this to other filmmakers or critics. Fuelers aren't film producers. They've never been involved in anything like this before and they're honestly excited. Show them *something*. Trust me on this. You want them bragging about this to their pals at the country club.

If you'd like to see the zero-budget concept trailer created for *Orphaned Courage*, check out the book extras by visiting **www.josiahstendel.com/ filmfuelextras**.

Here are a few pointers when creating your proof of concept. To make it more manageable for you, consider filming it in an afternoon or over the weekend using resources already available to you. Unless you're my industry friend and have access to a dozen or more tanks, keep the trailer simple. Stupidly simple.

If you're already crewed up, pitch your team the idea of a concept trailer and see who's game. To simplify logistics, consider locations you already have access to or have used in the past. You don't want any surprises.

If you're already into production, you've got it easy—cut together a teaser from the dailies.

If you need a few extra hands behind the camera (or some extras in front of the camera), you may be able to utilize volunteers. Consider searching for charity-focused Greek life organizations at your local university. Alternatively, if you chose a local cause to support, reach out to the organization and see if they could help you round up some volunteer production assistants. Consider royalty-free stock music instead of a custom composition to keep finishing costs down in post-production.

When it comes to the script, choose bits from your film that are easy to shoot and combine them into a high-octane montage. A supercut of these shots will excite potential Fuelers to action. Keep in mind that you will be presenting this trailer to Fuelers in the middle of their business— where there will be potential distractions and background noise. Plan accordingly. I would avoid scenes relying heavily on dialogue or taking place in low light. Choose dramatic, high-contrast visuals that are sure to stand out in any environment.

If the POC process seems like a waste of time, consider that you could use many of the trailer shots in the final film. We certainly did. Nearly 90% of the clips in the *Orphaned Courage* proof of concept made it into the final edit. Keeping this in mind, you could intentionally choose a sequence that could serve double-duty—appearing in your proof of concept and your final film.

Don't be surprised if some Fuelers have their checkbook out before you can even show them the proof of concept. That's the power of the FilmFuel system. However, don't view the POC as any less valuable. When they see the teaser, they'll want to see the rest. They will visualize their name in the credits—their logo at the premiere. The wheels start to turn and their involvement starts feeling inevitable.

It's the clincher. The icing on the cake. Your slam-dunk.

Show them the trailer, and it's nothing but net.

Concept trailers are even more vital for young filmmakers. The proof of concept shows these established (often older) businesspeople that you're not just a kid with a phone making a home movie but that this legit production is already underway. Young filmmakers must portray conviction in their abilities to get Fuelers to invest in their dreams. And the best way to amp up and display your confidence? Have something besides words and paper to show for it.

26
STORYBOARDS

If you've already created storyboards or other previsualization materials, dust 'em off and show 'em off in your pitch. If you don't have storyboards, consider finding a local artist who can help you develop a few. Instead of storyboarding the entire film, consider creating boards for a few key moments or the scenes portrayed in the proof of concept trailer. It's not a must, but it becomes another exciting visual element to help pitch your film and the passion behind it to these Fuelers.

Ultimately, you want an overflow of creative materials. Having all these options makes it a cinch to tailor your pitch to the personality of the person across from you. Are they more interested in the financials? Focus on the One-Sheet and budget breakdown. Do they want to watch the trailer again and again? Get them even more excited by showing them the script and storyboards too.

If you're a little uneasy about pitching businesses, that's okay! Use these support materials to get out of speaking the whole time. If you go in with *only* your Quick Pitch (discussed in Chapter 29), the onus is on you to present your project convincingly.

GULP. "WHAT IF I FORGET A CRUCIAL DETAIL?"

If you have a trailer and some pre-written information, you let your tools do the talking.

These visuals not only present your project persuasively and thoroughly (your One-Sheet won't forget a single detail), but they also give you a chance to breathe, regain your composure, and consider what to say next.

27| THE FILMFUEL SECRET

This next section is the most critical part of this entire book.

No joke. This is the core of FilmFuel. This is why it works. Commit this to memory and enjoy the rewards. To persuade Fuelers to get involved, present your project as a **win-win-win**. These three wins are the three reasons (and only three reasons) businesses will part with their hard-earned cash to fuel your film.

The first reason is the cause. As we discussed earlier, businesses want to give evidence of their humanity. They get to make a difference by raising money and awareness for the cause you chose to attach to your film. The cause you are personally motivated to support. Win.

The second reason is the film itself. Chances are, this Fueler has never been a part of the motion picture industry before. They get to do something they can brag about to their golf buddies—double win.

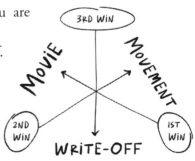

But if that's all we're bringing to the table, very few businesses will bite. I mean, it's all fine and good, but at this point, they're still asking, "So what?" There's no tangible benefit for them worthy of their commitment. Here's the secret sauce to change that—the third win.

The win for the business is that the Fueler can empower our dreams and make a difference, yes, but they can also write off their contribution. *Wait a second—they can do WHAT?*

To make it valuable for the business, you want to make it possible for the Fueler to deduct the funds they give you as a business expense. Now you *could* create a non-profit (challenging) or pursue Fiscal Sponsorship (messy), but by far, the best way I've discovered to do so is this. *Offer to put their logo in the credits of the film. In exchange for the promotion, they can deduct the monies paid to you as an advertising expense.* Additionally, if you are putting together a legacy premiere, include in your advertising offer that you will promote them from the stage and on any materials (brochures, t-shirts, banners, etc.) associated with the event.

This is the only time paying with exposure works. Because you're advertising for them, the business can write off the contribution—much like they can write off the expense of putting their logo on the local sports team's jerseys.

Clever, huh?

The IRS refers to this practice as "goodwill advertising." As it was explained to me by several accountants and attorneys, a business expense must be considered ordinary and necessary to be deductible. If there is a reasonable expectation of future business (for example, your film being shown in the same geographic region as the Fueler's business), it would likely qualify the expense of advertising in a film's credits as *necessary* by IRS standards. Although the placement of the brand's logo in the credits is an "out-of-the-box" promotion, advertising in unique ways to generate awareness and future business is itself a commonly accepted business practice, fulfilling the *ordinary* standard of a deductible expense.

Before putting the Third Win into practice, please be responsible and consult a licensed professional. Remember, I'm recounting my personal experience here. Tax laws are in constant flux and depending on what part of the world you find yourself in, these laws may prevent you from applying this Third Win.

One additional word of caution, avoid supporting any political parties or candidates with your film. At the time of writing, in the United States, businesses may not expense any contributions that directly or indirectly benefit a specific politician or political party.

Because this Third Win is the fulcrum of the FilmFuel method, make sure the details are legally squared away before continuing. This stuff gets complicated quickly, so it is always worth a consultation with your accountant or a qualified professional if you have any doubts. If you get a thumbs-up from them, as I did, this can be a straightforward and lucrative way of presenting your film as a marketing opportunity and a win-win-win for businesses.

If you live outside of the United States or your accountant expresses any concerns about applying this method under the jurisdiction of your local tax code, share with them your reasoning behind it. Explain that you're offering advertising space to the entity in your film's credits—a legitimate business expense.

If your accountant has second thoughts, ask them to help you find a way to make it more inviting for businesses to partner with you. "*How could I present this so that the opportunity is also beneficial for the contributing company?*" might be a helpful question for them. Perhaps they'll let you in on some other ways to make the Third Win work for your locale—things you'd need to include in your pitch or in your film to make them compliant.

Usually, by this point in your pitch, the Fueler has already made up their mind as to whether they plan to contribute to you or not. The Third Win may not turn a no into a yes, but it helps those who react positively to justify the expense to themselves and their business partners.* It allows them to take the leap and commit by answering the "So what?" question hanging out in the back of their minds.

---

* Remember how important it is to first sell with emotion and then to supply logical evidence to reaffirm their decision? Review the second half of Chapter 24 for more about the *Emotional Reasoning Theory.*

With the approval of your accountant, channeling the Third Win into your FilmFuel pitch is the secret to make partnering with your film extremely lucrative for potential Fuelers. They're thinking, *"I get to be a part of a movie, change lives, and benefit my business at the same time? What an irresistible offer!"*

28|
ADVERTISING AGREEMENT

The last pitch material you need to bring with you is a super simple contract. If a Fueler contributes to your film in exchange for advertising in the credits, you need to get something in writing—remember the lesson I learned from my "electrons" situation?

But contracts are such a headache, Josiah!

They don't have to be. For this, simple works great. How simple? According to the lawyers we consulted, your contract might be as straightforward as, "Contributor Company pays $5000.00 for advertisement in the film credits and at the film premiere of This Amazing Film by Production Company." The two main elements to include in the agreement are agreed-upon services (with the word *advertising* or *advertisement*) and the amount. Instead of the names in the example, have blanks that you can fill out for each Fueler.

Print out a stack of copies and carry them in your pitch materials. When a Fueler wants to participate, bust out a copy, sign, and date it. Then have the business owner countersign. If possible, take a photo of the signed document (with the check beside it) and give them the original copy to file away. That's it!

Again, get the advice of a licensed professional to make sure that in your jurisdiction, this signed document is enough evidence to substantiate a business expense.

Whew! I know that was a lot of legalese, and I'm sorry. Not to worry— the details will be here for you whenever you need a refresher.

We now know the Fuelers to approach, the materials we need, and the secret to making an irresistible offer. What I want to explore with you next is how to put the pieces together so that you can pitch your project with confidence.

» TAKE ACTION » » » » » » » »

✓ **Make your list of potential Fuelers.** If your charity handed you a list, start with that. If not, list every business owner with whom you have a *personal connection*. These could include restaurants, insurance agents, dentists, orthodontists, car dealerships, dry cleaners, accountants, supermarkets, real estate agents, retail outlets, and any others that come to mind.

✓ **Next, double the size of your list.** If your list feels short, continue by adding friends or family in your network who may themselves have some personal connections to business owners. Order your list by closest connections—those most likely to help you—putting those at the top.

✓ **Finally, collect or create your pitch materials.** These include a sponsor One-Sheet, proof of concept, advertising agreement, and storyboards. Remember, downloadable versions are available at **www.josiahstendel.com/filmfuelextras**. If needed, set aside a few days this week to complete your pitch materials. It'll be worth every minute.

PART 4

SHOOT
YOUR
SHOT

29| THE QUICK PITCH

Imagine you're in Los Angeles visiting some friends. It's been a long day, and you're absolutely beat. UGH. What a relief to see the hotel lobby—you're almost to your room. As you step into the elevator and the doors start to close, a man throws his hand between the doors. "Wait!"

C'mon man, you think. *Just get the next one.* You roll your eyes. *Could this day get any longer?* However, as this man steps into the elevator, you realize he looks kind of familiar.

All at once, it hits you.

Oh my goodness. It's Jerry Bruckheimer.

This is your chance. Your one shot.

Gulp.

This could be a career-making or career-breaking opportunity. You've got 45 seconds until the elevator reaches your floor, but you have no idea if he'll get out first.

What will you do? What will you say?

Although I can't promise a meeting with Jerry Bruckheimer any time soon, I can promise you this. If you create your power-packed pitch like the one described in the next few chapters, most people you encounter will join the crusade.

The Script

The first step of the Quick Pitch (or QP) is to introduce yourself and build rapport. Tell them **who** you are. Tell them how much you love their product or how frequently you visit their establishment.

Second, tell them **what** you're doing there. Share about the film. Your logline should be no more than two sentences summarizing your story's key concept and conflict.

Third, tell them **why** you are doing this. Mention the cause and the connection to you—why you specifically want to support this cause.

Finally, tell them **how** you're going to make this happen. Here you'll put the ball into their court by sharing how Fuelers can get involved. Don't be afraid to make your ask. Remember the win-win-win in Chapter 27. I've used a specific phrase to communicate this call to action: "We've built the rocket; we just need the fuel to get us there." Tie it all together by explaining the Third Win—how it benefits the company.

Get across the idea that you've done all the legwork.

You simply need the fuel for your film to take off.

So, if I'm walking into a store, approaching the owner—what exactly should I say? How do I work my film into a normal conversation without feeling like I'm forcing it? How about I walk you through a brief example dialogue I modeled after some discussions with business owners.

YOU: [Introduce yourself/build rapport] Hey! I'm Josiah. You guys look busy today!

OWNER: Hey. Yeah, we sure are! What can I do for you?

YOU: I just had a quick question. Is it a good time?

OWNER: Sure, I've got a moment.

YOU: I'm a local filmmaker who's done [this cool project] and [that cool project—it's okay to name drop a little. Build credibility quickly], and I'm working on this new short film. It's about [LOGLINE], and I'm using it as a tool to raise money and awareness for [CAUSE]! It's something near and dear to my heart because [PERSONAL MOTIVATION], and I can't wait to get started.

OWNER: That's so cool!

YOU: We've built the rocket; now we're just looking for the fuel—businesses who will partner with us to make it happen. Here, let me show you the teaser trailer!

You pull out your phone and hit play.

OWNER: Whoa! That looks awesome! You mentioned you're looking for the fuel? How much do you guys need?

At this, you hand over the One-Sheet.

YOU: We already have [AMOUNT] committed, leaving about [AMOUNT] that we still need by [DEADLINE]* to make this film happen. But here's what we can offer in exchange: not only are you helping to make a film (already something special), but you're also changing the lives of [orphaned children/adorable puppies/insert the impact of your cause], *and* you can write the contribution off as an advertising expense!

OWNER: Wait, seriously?

YOU: Yes! In exchange for your help, we'll provide advertising services—promoting your business in the film's credits and at our film's premiere.

In response, the owner will likely ask a few questions. If the business is financially able to, the owner will pull out their checkbook. You've made it a no-brainer and they're ready to partner with you. Don't forget to grab the simple advertising agreement to seal the deal. It's also best to get their contact information with a promise of updates as you make the film.

After the Fueler agrees, sign and date the contract.

YOU: Here. Keep this for your records. Thank you so much for your time and contribution. I'm so excited to make a difference together!

OWNER: Totally. I love what you're doing and am glad to be a part. Have a good one!

Of course, not every conversation will run like this, and not every business owner will respond this favorably. We'll talk about what to do in those scenarios later. The flexibility to respond in the moment will come with practice. The script should merely give you an idea of pitch length, what to expect, and how to generally navigate the conversation.

---

* A healthy dose of urgency motivates action.

Honestly, if this whole pitching thing sounds scary, shake the jitters by practicing the script in front of the mirror a few times as you tailor it to your film. Make it fit you. Or grab a friend and practice with them.* You could even have them go off script and run a few sub-optimal scenarios past you— like the business owner who's having a crazy day, starts super skeptical, or gets distracted by an important phone call halfway through your spiel.

The more you can pitch your film, the easier and more natural it will be for you when you're in front of a Fueler for real. Your early pitches will also give you a mental library of "frequently asked questions" that you should address in future iterations of your script. Does the same question keep coming up? Revise your Quick Pitch to answer that question proactively. This will not only improve the clarity of your pitch but also address any potential concerns before they are raised.

While you want to be well-informed on important details, you will undoubtedly run into Fuelers with questions you don't know how to answer. It's important to be honest with them: *"You know what? That's a great question that I honestly don't know the answer to. Let me find out for you."*

After you've crafted your Quick Pitch, commit it to memory. It doesn't have to be word-perfect every time. After all, the next Fueler won't have a clue if you switched a word around from the last time you pitched it. Just make sure all the necessary information makes the cut.

The entire QP should be short. Thirty seconds, three minutes, five minutes— the exact length doesn't matter. The key? Don't give an eternal summary.

"Page one. It was a dark and stormy night—"

NO. Let me stop you right there.

I know your script is amazing, but busy business owners won't have time for that.

Keep it long enough to get the essential details in but short enough to keep their attention. Combining passion and brevity is the key to a

---

* Some FilmFuel filmmakers have found success with the following practice: try role-playing a completely impromptu pitch with a friend and record the audio on your phone. How would you casually describe the film you're creating? Once you've finished your ad-libbed attempt, transcribe the recording to give you a starting point for your official Quick Pitch script.

successful pitch.* The more respectful you can be of their time, the more likely they will be to forget about everything else and get crazy excited about your project. Don't ask me why, but it's true.

Be ready to share your QP with anybody—your cousin, the barista, or Jerry Bruckheimer. Always have your pitch on the tip of your tongue. Keep your pitch materials with you. Have a copy in your car or on your tablet. You never know when you might need it—the most funding comes from the most unexpected places. Remember my orthodontist?

---

* For even more on crafting a compelling pitch, check out "Good in a Room" by former MGM Director of Creative Affairs Stephanie Palmer.

30| YOUNG GUN ADVANTAGE

Many young filmmakers believe they won't be taken seriously in the industry until they've had decades of experience. Before we move on, I want to dispel that myth. If you're a young filmmaker—a high-school or college student—looking to do something big, you can absolutely use that in your Quick Pitch to your benefit.

It seems counterintuitive, right? You wouldn't necessarily think that being a young filmmaker would play to your advantage. In reality, your age can become a *selling point*. You could say something like, *"I want to show how young people like me can make a difference—that we can change the world with our ideas."*

Any decent human being will shove money in your face.

Although no teenager wants to emphasize how young they are, doing so can create tremendous momentum for your project. When someone young decides to channel their energy into making a difference, it is truly something special.

How special?

I remember my experience of casting the lauded actor John Wells (*One Must Fall, Wolf Hound*) as the prodigal brother in *Orphaned Courage*. Since the production, we've become close friends. But the first day he joined us on set, I can't tell you how nervous I was. Not only was he the most recognizable face attached to the film, but we had only ever corresponded through text messages.

And my age never came up.

If I'm honest, I thought he would back out if it did.

As soon as John arrived on set and made me as the director, I saw his face fall.

I kicked myself inwardly. Who was I kidding? This guy was next level. And I expected *him* to work on *my* set? Although John was the epitome of professionalism, I trudged through the rest of the film shoot on automatic.

Later that evening, I saw a notification that I had been tagged in a post. By John Wells, no less.

"So, I just now wrapped on a film—there's something extraordinary about it that I need to share.

The production was pleasant. Professional. More so than many. The filmmaker, writer, and director of the piece had a clear vision, was knowledgeable, professional, seemingly experienced, and technically savvy. Ambitious, talented, and personable. Well-spoken, and he controlled the set well enough. I like the guy.

The shots looked great. Dramatic. Plenty of coverage. Some impressive effects and choreography. Efficient use of funds, with outstanding production value considering the budget.

There were a few bumps and inefficiencies here and there, but no more than any other production I've been a part of, really. Morale stayed high, and the film never fell too far behind schedule that shots were dropped or compromised. I've been on plenty of significantly more amateur sets. This shoot was equivalent to some on which I've worked with ten, even twenty times more monetary value behind them.

All of that is good. Great. Cool.

But none of that is EXTRAORDINARY.

No. What was extraordinary was when I first arrived on set to discover that this filmmaker with whom I'd been conversing throughout preproduction—the writer, director, co-cinematographer, co-producer—was sixteen years old. Eat your hearts out, filmmakers. Eyes on Josiah Stendel. This kid has a future."

From a young age, we try to hide what makes us different. *Be like everybody else,* we think. *Don't stand out. Don't call attention to yourself.*

But really, blending in is a mistake. And we spend the rest of our adult lives trying to unlearn it. What will get an employer to choose you? Standing out. What will get your film funded? Standing out. It's not copying someone else that leads to happiness. No—*confidence in your God-given uniqueness does.* The earlier you can embrace it, the earlier you will experience the benefits. Being a young person who's driven to do something meaningful with their life is extraordinary. If someone wants to put your brace-face on a billboard? Gosh darn it, let them! Don't let insecurity stand between you and a fully funded film. There's unbelievable enthusiasm for young people. Capitalize on it.

Maybe you are reading this and not high school or college-aged—don't fret. You're not an old fogey who missed the boat. There's no age limit or requirement for FilmFuel. I simply wanted to show how, if that *is* you, your young age can help you win extra favor with the Fuelers you approach. At FilmFuel, we call it the *Young Gun Advantage.*

31| QUICK PITCH POINTERS

When it comes to successfully pitching businesses, your *timing* matters most.

If you enter a business and there's a long line, or you see staff running around under a lot of stress, come back later or make an appointment. If the environment is consistently hectic, regardless of the time you're there, consider moving on to the next lead on your list. Chaotic environments counteract the trust and rapport you need to build with your potential Fueler. If you're taking someone's attention away from a customer, I guarantee they won't be thinking about your film—their mind will be on the money they just missed out on.

To increase your chances of success, first, visit as a customer. See what the atmosphere of the business is like. Is the work environment high-stress or more relaxed and casual? Is there a lull in the flow of customers where it might be a good time to speak to them? Timing, many times, will make the difference between hearing a yes or a no.

Timing, timing, timing.

Here's another secret I uncovered after weeks of approaching businesses. Want to increase your chances of success? Go on sunny Fridays. Why sunny Fridays? When the weather is pleasant, there's a better chance the people will be, too. In addition, when the staff is nearing the freedom of the weekend, they are generally more upbeat and willing to help.

Sounds hokey, but it's true. Approach potential Fuelers on sunny Fridays, whenever possible. The flip side is that you want to avoid approaching Fuelers early in the week. Of course, rainy Mondays are even worse.

Make sure that your pitch is rooted in sincerity and empathy. Say it like you mean it. Better yet, *really mean it*. People can smell an agenda a mile away. If you're just in it for the money, Fuelers can tell. That doesn't mean you have to become a monk and rid yourself of all earthly possessions, but don't show up *just* for the money.

Sincerity is easiest when your cause deeply excites you. Find that genuine enthusiasm. Remember the idea of *passion transfer* from Chapter 22? If you lack excitement, Fuelers will too. To keep your energy high, try to visualize your passion pulling them on board during each pitch.

What If I Get a No?

It should be obvious, but don't be a jerk if you get a metaphorical door slammed in your face when approaching these Fuelers. Even if you are met with strong personalities, always remain gracious and professional. A few businesses I've pitched wouldn't even let me finish before they flatly stated, *"Nope, sorry. Not interested."* What do you do in that situation? Thank them for their time and move on.

Don't lose your cool. Keep your composure through your exit.

But Josiah, why not try to overcome their objections? If you want to clear up a misconception and they're willing to hear you out—go for it! But you're not a used car salesman trying to manipulate them into something "for only pennies a day." If they don't bite, throw 'em back.

It's kind of like having to convince someone to marry you.

Even if you win them over, do you want to be with someone you *talked into* loving you? You want passionate partners—in life and business.

If the Fueler isn't interested, that's fine. Find someone who is. There are so many more businesses you can approach that it's honestly not worth stressing over.

32 | WHAT ARE FRIENDS FOR

With actual Fuelers taking first place, the second most valuable resource for film funding is your friend circle. Remember, you will never be pitching your friends for funding directly. Instead, you'll be asking them to help *connect* you with Fuelers they know.

The QP for your friends will be very similar—you'll first build rapport, catch up, and small talk for a few moments (hopefully an easy step, since these are already friends and acquaintances). If you aren't as close to them, perhaps remind them **who** you are and how you know them. "Oh, hey! This is [NAME]. Do you remember me from [the conference last year/ Amy's party/second grade]?"

Next, tell them **what** your film is about. "The reason I'm calling you is this. I'm making a film about [LOGLINE]." Then, transition to **why** you're doing this project. Mention the cause and your personal connection to it. Then, tell your friend **how** you're approaching businesses for funding and the way it benefits them with a win-win-win. Clarify that you're not calling to ask for money. If it fits your style, crack a joke about them breathing a sigh of relief. Instead, you're making it possible for businesses to contribute to your project in exchange for advertising.

Conclude by asking them if they know anyone who might be able to help you.

"I've gone through my personal list, and I'm out of businesses to ask. Is there anybody that you know that I should reach out to? Anybody that you think might be interested in something like this?" Give them a moment. Let them fill the silence. If they have trouble thinking of anyone, share a few businesses that have already contributed or begin to list out some ideas—much like I did earlier. Ask them who their dentist is, who they get their insurance through, or if they know any real estate agents closely.

You want to hear something like, "Oh yeah, you should talk to my cousin Danny. He runs the local florist shop. Here's his number."

If your friends are a tech-savvy bunch, you can also text, email, or message them via social media. Explain your project and tell them that you're looking for businesses that want to make a difference in the community. Then ask if they can think of anyone who might be willing to help.

This next part will sound like a "duh," but I'm always surprised at how many forget this critical detail. Later, when you reach out to these businesses, mention the mutual friend who recommended them. With your buddy's permission, piggyback off their credibility. Whenever you can truthfully say that someone they know sent you, it'll build instant rapport and give the Fueler a reason to drop what they're doing and listen. It's kind of like becoming immediate friends because of the friend you have in common. It's pretty cool.

After your friend has given you some people to reach out to, you'll want to (at least low-key) ask for permission to use their name. You could either do this with a flat-out question ("Can I tell them you sent me?") or as more of a statement ("Okay, awesome. I'll be in touch with them. I'll tell them you sent me. Thank you so much.") that they could correct if they didn't want you to do so.

33| YOUR FIRST FIVE PITCHES

There's a great story from the gold rush days about a young guy who sold everything he had to go out West and join the fray.

He was all in.

But after a few frustrating weeks of finding nothing, he decided to call it quits and recoup what he could by selling his mine for cash and his equipment for scrap. The proprietor of the local junkyard, excited by the gold-hunting gear, asked some local miners for advice and soon realized the young man hadn't cut far enough into the rock.

He went back to the mine and struck gold—three feet further than the young man had been willing to go.

If you throw in the towel and walk away after your first pitch, convinced it's not working and you'll never get funding, you're abandoning all the effort you've put in—three feet from striking gold. It's essential to look at the first few pitches as practice.

You're just warming up.

Let finding success in your first few pitches be a pleasant surprise if it happens, rather than an expectation that leads to disappointment if it doesn't.

One word of caution, if you've gone more than five pitches without even the slightest nibble, I would advise re-evaluating your pitch, your logline, and your strategy. Look for what's making people bail. Is it the content, timing, or delivery? Ask some friends in the industry for their feedback— or video your best pitch and send it to me.

If you're struggling to deliver a confident presentation, consider teaming up with someone who might be more comfortable and composed in front of others. There's no shame in pitching as a duo.

Don't be too hard on yourself if your first pitch or two go nowhere. As you gain experience, these conversations will become more natural, and your confidence will grow. Eventually, you will have people on the edge of their seats. Don't give up.

Perfect is the Enemy of Good

Don't wait until your QP is perfectly polished before pitching it to anyone. Instead, keep tweaking and improving your pitch as you start using it. You'll spontaneously add something, get an amazing response, and think to yourself, *"Why haven't I said that before?"* It happens all the time.

Or maybe you'll notice you lose people's attention on the same sentence every time. If so, simply rework that line to keep them engaged.

Notice what questions you get asked after each pitch. Is it something you already covered in your pitch? If so, try tweaking your QP to address that concern more effectively for the next person you pitch.

Pitching involves continuous testing and tweaking. But you can't tweak if you aren't testing.

It reminds me of getting thrown from a jet ski for the first time. Unlike driving a car, you can only turn a jet ski while accelerating. It sounds like a no-brainer, but it's scarily counter-intuitive for beginners. If you let off the gas and try to turn the handles to make a sharp turn, you'll keep moving in the same direction you were already going. Which is scary if you want to avoid a collision of Titanic proportions. However, if you throttle the engine up instead, you'll make hairpin turns without incident.

What's the point? You can only course-correct as you get moving. Your pitch will continually improve as you start giving it.

Don't wait for a flawless script. Done is better than perfect.

34| WHAT HAPPENS AFTER

Whether or not a Fueler commits to your project, end your interaction by asking for referrals. Business owners know business owners. Especially locally.

Even if a Fueler hands you a no instead of a check, a good way of keeping your momentum going would be to ask, *"Do you know any other local businesses who might want to support something like this?"* You may even tug on their heartstrings a little by bringing up the cause one last time: *"Do you know anybody else who might want to help bring orphans into loving Kentucky homes of their own?"* Oftentimes, the resulting recommendations are the lifeblood that keeps your funding process rolling.

Don't be surprised if they refer you to a business that has already contributed to you! Business owners know each other better than you do. Whether it's a new idea or not, always treat it like the best idea ever. They're trying to be helpful! Even if they try to send you somewhere you've already been, take it as confirmation that you're on the right track.

You just made it through the toughest part of FilmFuel Bootcamp. Congratulations! Now you know the secrets of pitching Fuelers and walking away fueled. No more waiting on studios or producers to greenlight your production. You have the power to greenlight yourself—*right now*!

I hope you feel inspired and ready to put these principles into practice.

After you approach the first business, go back to your list and repeat for the next one—and the one after that—until you're fully funded. The more time you have for this, the more you'll see the investment you put into preparation pay off. It's like filmmaking, right? The battle is won or lost in pre-production.

Get ready for some legwork. Sometimes you will have to approach a dozen or so businesses, but this methodology **simplifies the process** and creates **unbelievable** momentum. These Fuelers become part of your crew. They'll be cheering you on—supporting and promoting you from the sidelines as you do the same for them.

I love the timeless Silicon Valley adage: "*If you want advice, ask for money. If you want money, ask for advice.*" It's especially apropos when approaching friends with the FilmFuel framework. Instead of asking for money, ask for their advice. Ask them for introductions with Fuelers and watch the money follow. Doors will open in front of you as you attach your cause and put the FilmFuel process into practice.

Next, I want to open your eyes to the world of non-monetary support— things besides funding that Fuelers can contribute to your project. Don't let the title of the section scare you. Budget cuts don't have to be bad. By the end, you may only need half the funding you thought you did.

» TAKE ACTION » » » » » » »

Craft your Quick Pitch and grab your supporting materials. Use the example script in Chapter 29 to inspire the creation of your own film's Quick Pitch. Practice this in front of the mirror or role-play it with a friend. Decide which support materials from Part 3 you will bring along. Then, ensure you have sufficient paper copies in your car and any visuals on a laptop or tablet ready to present. You should be getting excited. Fuel is coming!

Start your engines. Finding funding will be easiest if you *finish the rest of the book first.* There are some secrets to sustainability that I still want to show you. But if you're raring to go and feel ready to collect some FilmFuel, now's the time to pull out the list you created at the end of Part 3 and reach out to your first Fueler.

If possible, make contact on a sunny Friday and pitch your film in person. Don't forget to bring up the Third Win from Chapter 27. If all goes well, you'll walk away with a check and recommendations for more businesses to approach.

If not, though, remember—that's okay. Congratulate yourself on the practice round, and move on to the next Fueler on your list. Rinse and repeat until your film has a budget.

PART 5

THE
BUDGET
CUT

35| THE PIZZA TEST

Feeding our crew of 40 people three full meals per day for eight days *should* have cost over $10,000. Maybe even as much as $15,000 by some estimates.

Do you know how much it ended up costing us?

Nothing.

Not one cent.

Why? Because I discovered the power of non-monetary support—things Fuelers provide besides dollars in the bank to make your film possible. Sometimes a business will genuinely want to help you but won't be at a place where they can afford to write you a check. Thankfully, some of the most valuable help comes in a different form.

These resources will help you stretch your funding in ways you never thought possible so that you can spend every dollar where it matters most. In that sense, a budget cut is a beautiful thing. By the end of this section, you may only need half the money you thought. Maybe even less.

Ready to get saving?

FILM FUEL – THE LIFE-CHANGING FILM FUNDING SECRET

Would You Like Fries With That?

One of the most important items on an indie film budget also happens to be one of the most expensive and often overlooked. Craft services—the food catered to talent and crew during production.

Having worked on independent films for a decade and counting, I have heard dozens of horror stories related to food on set. Although I wish these incidents were the exception rather than the rule, the countless complaints from resentful cast and crew reveal reality. Crafty ends up as an afterthought in most independent productions. But what filmmakers don't realize is that quality meals keep your crew happy.

Josiah, what's wrong with pizza?

Well, nothing. Because feeding a large group with a few boxes is cheap and easy, most low-budget productions grab a few pizzas and call it a day. And every so often, fast-food pizza is tasty. But imagine eating that every day, all day, for a week-long shoot. And then moving on to the next set just to see—you guessed it—more pizza! Several crew members on my team recalled such scenarios.

I call this indicator of filmmaker thoughtfulness the *pizza test*.

It's not that pizza is terrible; it's just the bare minimum.

As directors and producers, it is our responsibility to take good care of our cast and crew. They're putting in long hours for us. The least we can do is make sure they stay well-fueled. Especially if you're applying the FilmFuel method to a short, low-budget production, there's a good chance some of your cast and crew will be volunteering their time or doing you a favor with reduced rates.

These people believe the most in you and your vision and are pouring their blood, sweat, and tears into making your film. As a decent human being, it's your responsibility to go beyond the bare minimum and make production an enjoyable experience for them. What do cast and crew want to eat? Ideally, something homemade.

Now you might be thinking, *"Do I look like a chef to you? There is no way I can afford gourmet cooking for my cast and crew!"* I get it. You likely don't have the time (or culinary chops) to put together an exquisite buffet. And the alternative, having crafty catered, is guaranteed to blow your indie budget. But not to fear, FilmFuel is here.

With a cause attached, there's a good chance supportive Fuelers will provide craft services. For *Orphaned Courage*, local restaurants joined forces to provide over ten thousand dollars worth of meals at no cost to our team whatsoever.

What if I could show you how to pull that off for your next film?

Even better, this approach to catering is evergreen. These restaurants will provide food for more than just your current project. With FilmFuel, this network of assistance will also sustain your future films. You will be able to revisit these Fuelers with other opportunities and quickly round up the resources you need to make those films a reality.

36| GETTING CRAFTY

So, how do you pass the *pizza test?*

How do you secure quality craft services without breaking the bank?

In Parts 3 and 4, we discussed approaching businesses for financial fuel. Although there are a few key differences, the general process should sound familiar.

When you approach restaurants, target casual dining chains like Panera Bread and Chick-fil-A (two of our key Fuelers). Ask around in your friend circles to discover possible connections to the franchise's manager or owner. Then use the Chapter 29 Quick Pitch formula to share your project, cause, and motivation with that person.

Remember the Third Win from Chapter 27? You advertise for the Fueler in your film's credits so that they can write the expense off their taxes. This strategy turned heads when I approached Fuelers for *financial* support. Thinking restaurants would be just as excited by the proposal, I emphasized the Third Win to them in my first few pitches.

But something strange happened. I didn't get much of a reaction.

Here's what I learned.

Most restaurants are regularly asked to give away food for promotional purposes. For example, your local 5K run has dozens of sponsors on its banners. Many of the sponsors? Local restaurants. Because they're familiar with being approached, I found it wildly more effective to emphasize *the cause* over the Third Win.

Although they may not care about writing off the endeavor as an advertising expense, they highly value the exposure of a logo placement in the credits. It makes sense. When they cater an event, their logo will typically be displayed somewhere—on the back of a t-shirt, inside a brochure, or on event signage. In the same way, communicate that you'll put the restaurant's logo in the credits (and wherever else you'll promote your Fuelers) as a thank you.

Next, discuss how many meals you need to cover and ask if the restaurant would be willing to help provide a few of them.

That's the trick with this.

Most restaurants are willing to help and can contribute at least *some* food, but unless you're a team of two filming a one-day shoot, it is unlikely that a single restaurant will be able to cater the *entire* production. Don't arrive at the restaurant asking them to supply all the meals—rookie mistake. To get everything provided for you, use multiple caterers. Patchwork style.

For example, with *Orphaned Courage*, Panera Bread covered breakfasts, while Chick-fil-A supplied our warm meals. We patched together a meal plan so that no one restaurant was responsible for all the food. If you have a smaller cast and crew, you might be able to get away with only one caterer, but why stop there? Getting different restaurants on board provides variety and a wonderful experience for your hard-working team. And all it costs is a little legwork.

37 | TIME FOR LUNCH

Want to know the secret to getting meals provided?

In the early days of FilmFuel, I left several restaurant pitches empty-handed and confused. *"Why am I running into so many closed doors?"* I thought. Then, one of the casual dining joints dropped a bombshell. I was too late.

Restaurants, coffee shops, and bakeries have a budgeted amount of their product to give away for promotional and charitable purposes.

Wait. Did you get that? They set aside food *for people like you*! If nothing else gives you the confidence to walk into establishments boldly and tell them about your film, that should.

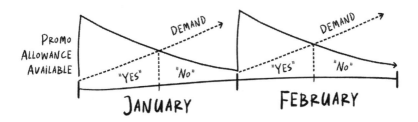

But if you pitch restaurants toward the end of the month, like I did, or shortly before your production, there's a good chance you'll be turned down. Why? The franchise will have already used up its monthly giveaway allowance. When I revisited the same venues at the start of the next month—boom—we secured meals.

Make sure you pitch the restaurant *at the beginning of the month*. If possible, even a month or two before your production. The bigger your ask, the more advance notice will help.

Restaurant vs. Restaurant

Another pro tip? Elicit friendly competition.

Once you get your first restaurant onboard, casually name-drop in your next pitch. For example, if Panera just agreed to contribute some bagels and bread, I might say, "Panera is helping us out with breakfast. Could you help us out with dinner?" Name-dropping other contributors adds credibility and sprinkles in a healthy dose of competition. Don't be surprised if that next restaurant nonchalantly tries to one-up the other contributor.

In Chapter 13, we discussed that businesses are eager to demonstrate their humanity. They're not all money-hungry capitalists. This holds true for restaurants as well. They may even one-up each other to become the top sponsor for the charitable event.

With catering, you will reach critical mass early. The first commitment is the hardest, but once you gain momentum, the remaining meals will come together quickly and easily.

When organizing meals for your production, keep in mind your cast and crew's dietary restrictions and allergies. Ask them first so you are armed with any special requests when restaurants ask. You want to avoid the awkwardness of proudly serving chicken nuggets to a vegan film crew.

I'm sorry, okay? I didn't know chickens had feelings. Please stop crying, man.

Think Ahead

Set your sights on the big picture. What do I mean by that? Don't restrict the help of these restaurants to your film shoot only. When we created our legacy premiere for *Orphaned Courage*, all the catering for the event was also gifted to us. It was a ton—finger foods and desserts for more than fifty VIP guests. All supplied for free.

If the restaurant cannot contribute meals to production, ask about involving them down the road. You could tell them, "We will be hosting a red-carpet premiere to raise money for [CAUSE] later this year. Could I revisit this with you then? Would you guys be willing to help with that?"

The takeaway here applies to all types of non-monetary support. Think ahead, and maybe you'll be able to turn a *no* into a *not yet.*

38|

LOCATION, LOCATION, LOCATION

Sage low-budget filmmaking advice is to write for what you have. But every time I hear someone say it, I want to tackle them—kindly. It's not wrong to write within your means. On the contrary, as Robert Rodriguez proved with *El Mariachi* (and the Weavers with *Cosmos*), planning to include what you have access to is smart filmmaking.

Unfortunately, I see so many neglecting their chief resource: *their network*.

Picture this: it's the swingin' 60s in Omaha, Nebraska. You just opened a package sent to you by some stranger—a cat named Stanley Milgram. *Far out, man.* Inside the mystery package is an explanation. Milgram intentionally sent this to a complete stranger to prove we're all connected in surprising ways. The instructions challenge the recipient to forward the package to anyone they knew who might be closer to Milgram's friend in Boston.

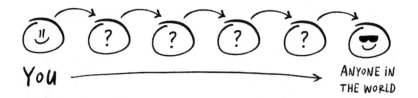

And you know what?

It only took six people to get that package to its intended destination.

He repeated this experiment again. And again. Each time, the chain consisted of no more than a half-dozen people. This became known as the *Six Degrees of Separation Theory*, which suggests that every person on the planet is only six connections away from anyone else. That means you're just a few friend-of-a-friend introductions away from rubbing elbows with the Pope. Or Tom Cruise. Or a long-lost relative.*

So, if we can reach anyone in the world through six people, why aren't we trying?

That's the problem. Most filmmakers have no idea what lies just beyond reach. You can have access to so much more—*just by asking*. For my short films, I've been able to get police officers with squad cars, K-9 units, ambulances, airports, and airplanes.

Did it cost me anything?

No.

Was it something I *had* before I asked?

Definitely no.

Did it elevate my film when I did ask?

Heck yes.

That's the secret. Don't write for what you have. Write for what you might be able to get. Be realistic when writing locations into your film to help manage costs—in other words, try to avoid writing "EXT. SPACE STATION" as a slugline unless you're pals with Elon. Just don't limit your options by refusing to explore them. Doors open when you ask for help.

---

* As a thought experiment, I analyzed my own network. I was stunned to discover I'm a mere two handshakes away from Pope Francis. And three from Tom Cruise.

A pivotal scene in *Orphaned Courage* takes place in an abandoned warehouse. I had never filmed in a location like that before and honestly had no clue where I could find one. Twelve days from production, we still had no leads.

So, I decided to ask my friends. In literally every conversation, I would work in this strange request, "Do you know anybody with connections to a run-down, warehouse-looking place?"

For the most part, I got weird looks in return.

But finally, I hit paydirt.

One of my friends knew the mayor of a neighboring town (what are the odds!) with an abandoned warehouse we could film in. For context, this neighboring town has a sizeable film school. Many students over the years had tried to film in this space but had always been refused permission. Some even trespassed and filmed without consent, leading to a general distaste of filmmakers on the property.

With one five-minute phone call, all that red tape vanished.

The mayor loved the cause-driven perspective of our film project and helped us secure the proper permissions before the end of the day. Not only did access to that location provide immense production value, but it became one of my favorite environments of the entire film.

As an aside, I recounted this experience to the film school faculty. They shook their heads in disbelief. "Josiah, there is no way you should have gotten to film there. Our students have been trying for years."

The impossible became possible for us.

All because we had a cause attached and simply asked.

39| LEAVE HOLLYWOOD. NO, SERIOUSLY.

Many filmmakers think high-quality filming locations will always demand payment. That's a myth. I have *never* had to pay a location fee. Finding the person responsible for giving permission can take some time, sure, but not once have I been charged to film somewhere.

Yes, some locations require permits,* but if you find that people in charge of locations are quoting rental fees, you're likely in a filmmaking hotspot like Atlanta, San Francisco, Los Angeles, or New York City. Lots of people are likely approaching these businesses for the use of their location. It's not a novelty for them.

What do they do? Naturally, they want to make a buck.

How can you avoid this? Find businesses that appreciate the excitement. Turning their establishment into a film set should be an exciting novelty for Fuelers. Not an intrusion so regular they've decided to monetize it.

Try filming in smaller towns a few hours away from these hotspots.

---

* It's your responsibility to figure this out *before* you use the location.

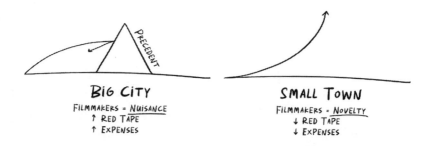

BIG CITY
FILMMAKERS = NUISANCE
↑ RED TAPE
↑ EXPENSES

SMALL TOWN
FILMMAKERS = NOVELTY
↓ RED TAPE
↓ EXPENSES

But, Josiah! I thought Hollywood was the goal! As filmmakers, shouldn't we want to be in the big city? It seems counterintuitive, right? But if you can convince your team of the merits, you will find your resources stretching much farther in smaller towns. Go small to go big.

Many filmmakers think, "Oh man—if I could only make it to Hollywood…" not realizing how challenging it is for non-studio filmmakers to stretch their limited resources in a major filmmaking hub. Why? Because of competition for resources.

Everyone is a filmmaker. Everyone is asking for these favors.

Which, in turn, drives the prices up.

True, you've got greater access to cast and crew in Los Angeles, but it's also a *red ocean.* A red ocean is an area or industry where the big players (the *sharks*) are already bloodying up the water with their hunt. It's too crowded. Instead, modern business wisdom says to find a *blue ocean.** Find a fresh, uncrowded corner of the industry where it's easier to stand out. The same is true for independent filmmaking.

Making big waves is easiest in small towns.

Do you think the mayor of Los Angeles would have given us an abandoned warehouse to use? There's no way. Would he even have given us the time of day to make our case? Unlikely. But because we live in a small town in the southeast, the doors of opportunity opened readily for us.

---

* To learn more about the power of differentiating yourself and your business, check out *Blue Ocean Strategy* by acclaimed strategy experts Chan Kim and Renée Mauborgne.

40| HOW TO PITCH FOR LOCATIONS

Still got that Quick Pitch top of mind? Good. It works with location managers too. In these situations, expect permission to film without fees and red tape. I never thought I could convince an airport to let me film a scene on their tarmac—chasing a plane as it took off. But when I showed up with my QP and a crazy ask, they said yes.

And I'm not the only one.

Armed with this same philosophy, friend and fellow low-budget filmmaker Dustin Lee got permission to film at one of the most high-security locations in the country—Hoover Dam—which is right up there with The Capitol Building and The White House. No civilians are allowed anywhere near the Dam's base or in the spillway tunnels running alongside it.

Dustin heads up Maple Films, a spirited indie film collective based out of Cleveland, Ohio. Taped to his monitor are the inspired words of screenwriter John Milius: *"Write what you want to see."* These simple words compelled him to write the Hoover Dam into his ambitious post-apocalyptic film series. "It was honestly a pipe dream," he told me. But as a year passed and the project materialized with a successful Kickstarter campaign, Dustin realized the only hurdle between him and the coolest footage of his career was a crazy ask.

Gulp.

"After scouring the Bureau of Reclamations website, I drafted a lengthy email introducing myself and my project. I attached every pitch material I could think of—down to a storyboarded sequence of shots," Dustin recalls.

Shockingly, they said yes.

Not just to filming on the water at the Dam's base, but even in the spillway tunnels. The Bureau coordinator assigned to the project pointed out just how special this was: "Because of security risks, you're on a very short list of people who have ever set foot in here. I've never been allowed in the tunnels, and I've worked at Hoover Dam for years." When I asked Dustin why he thinks *Evenfall* got the green light, he replied with a laugh, "You don't get what you don't ask for! Although filming at the Dam was the stuff of my dreams, I made sure our ask was practical.* No pyrotechnics, stunts off the Dam, or anything like that. Just two boats in the water."

Never be afraid to ask. You can always settle for smaller or simpler if you get a no. But chances are, if you reach for something insane, you'll get a whole lot farther than if you simply wrote for what you already had available to you.

It's only impossible until it isn't.

Your chances of success go way up when you can bring value to the filming locations. Although these Fuelers are not contributing *money* (so ditch the advertising expense component of the Third Win), they will be thrilled about the possible exposure for their business. To highlight this, you might say, "If we get permission to film here, we'll be happy to include your logo in the credits to share the spotlight with you." In this way, permitting you to film in their establishment benefits their visibility to customers.

---

* Dustin also obtained production insurance, without which he says his request would have been denied. Although to some, it may seem like an insignificant line item for an indie, insurance is critical for accessing off-limits locations like Hoover Dam. It gives those in charge peace of mind and instantly legitimizes your production—no matter how big or small.

Keep in mind that these locations are not soundstages. More than likely, this location is an active place of business. Unless you're prepared to pay them for lost business, don't ask them to shut down for a day so that you can film. They won't do it. That would be an instance they would rightfully expect payment.

Instead, the smart FilmFuel filmmaker will work with their schedule, not against it.

Find days and times these places are already closed. For example, many restaurants close on Sundays. If you're filming at a school or campus, aim for weekends and breaks in the academic calendar. If the location is open seven days a week, try filming after-hours or before opening.

Now, I'm gonna be your mom for a second.

This is important.

Since you're not only representing yourself and the film community but also a charitable cause, be on your best behavior in these locations. Again, it's a place of business. Make an extra effort to clean up after your cast and crew, leaving the area better than you found it.

In indie filmmaking, your reputation will always be your biggest asset. As soon as you plant your flag as a filmmaker fueling change, your community will take notice. Businesses will remember you. Think long-term.

Most local business owners know each other.

If you're not easy to work with or trash the place, the incident will negatively affect your reputation and future ability to find funding and locations. Yes, an accident—like a broken light fixture or scuffed wall—could be costly to remedy. But if you don't, the damage to your reputation will cost you even more.

Making an extra effort to leave every space better than you found it will create immeasurable goodwill with Fuelers.

To recap, be resourceful with locations. Just because something isn't necessarily the perfect location doesn't mean with a bit of creativity, it can't be. If you see somewhere you'd like to film, track down the person responsible for the space and explain the heart behind the project. With the FilmFuel framework, you'll be surprised what you can make use of for free.

41| LEARJETS AND ARMY FATIGUES

If you've ever wanted to fly in a private jet, FilmFuel is your ticket.

Although perhaps less obvious, providing special vehicles for your films is another way Fuelers can lend you support. Off the top of my head, my productions have included cop cars, SWOT and K-9 vehicles, ambulances, and airplanes—tiny Cessna aircraft and beautiful private Learjets. These are major production-value amplifiers.

Those assets would be impressive in any independent film, but for a young'un with no pedigree? Absolute craziness.

Here again, you see the small-town advantage in play. Do you think the Los Angeles Police Department would ever give me the time of day? I mean, for non-criminal reasons? They're just too busy. In a small town, filmmaking is a novelty. Remember the emotional desire to stand in the Winner's Circle? People

(FREE STUFF)

(police officers included) are excited about the prospect, and you will find opportunities opening ahead of you.

How did we get access to these special vehicles?

We approached the local police department and EMS and told them about the project. Having the cause backing up your project paves the way for you. I honestly didn't think it would be possible to get a police car for my film, but I just thought, "Well, what do I have to lose?" And ten minutes later, we shook hands with the Sheriff and officially had an off-duty officer tasked with helping us out. With our actor in the backseat, the cop drove his squad car around the block—lights flashing and sirens blaring.

In real handcuffs, no less. *Method actors.*

I'm telling you this for one reason. If we hadn't stepped out of our comfort zone and asked, none of this would have been possible. Walking into a conversation with law enforcement might seem intimidating, but you can't overthink it. Everyone wants to be in a movie.

Costumes and Props

Another creative way Fuelers can propel your project is with costumes, props, and other assets. For example, when one of my short films required military uniforms, I decided to ask the local National Guard outpost for help. I walked in there, pitched my project, and asked if they had any spare fatigues. Although they turned me down—shocker—they suggested trying the local army surplus store. When we asked, the owners graciously let us borrow any outfits our cast needed.

Even crazier, we went to law enforcement and asked if there was any chance we could borrow tactical vests—*their* tactical vests. Incredibly, they obliged.

Let that sink in. We borrowed six real, bulletproof vests from local law enforcement. Crazy. As the officer loaded the vests from his trunk into ours, he said, "We only have five spares. Here—I'll give you mine. I haven't needed it in a while, so I should be fine." I wish this had a punchline, but all I could think about during production week was, *"Oh please, Lord, don't let him die because of my short film."*

At the end of the day, neither resource took up a penny of our production budget. It's another example of getting access to impossible resources—for free—with FilmFuel.

What about post-production? A pivotal scene in *Orphaned Courage* involved a burning building. There was fire coming out of the windows. Smoke billowing. The whole shebang.

Because of the film's charitable purpose, Rodolphe Pierre-Louis and Luke Thompson from ActionVFX graciously stepped in. If you've never heard of them or their company, stop reading this and look them up. They're the real deal. You can find their bullet hits, explosions, and debris in everything from *Stranger Things* to the *Marvel* franchise.

From their unparalleled visual mayhem, you might never have guessed they have hearts of gold. But when they heard about our film and cause, they gave us free rein and put their entire library of footage at our disposal. Because of their generosity, the scene became so much more believable. In addition, they drove from Johnson City, Tennessee, to support our film at the legacy premiere. I'm telling you, these guys are amazing. If you need any top-notch visual effects elements or training, give Rodolphe and Luke a shout. They're friends of FilmFuel, and their VFX assets are worth every penny.

42 | EQUIPMENT

One of the most valuable resources is one we have yet to cover.

Before you write off that dream camera package, try reaching out to equipment rental companies. Give them your Quick Pitch and ask if they would be willing to help you out. Especially if you have a history of renting with them in the past, they may surprise you with a comped rental. This is what happened with *Orphaned Courage*. Nearly all our gear—camera, support, and lighting—was generously lent to us.

Although borrowing from rental houses is *possible*, they are more likely to offer you a generous discount. For example, my buddy Paul Friedman, owner of LensProToGo, gave us an amazing deal on an anamorphic lens package for *The Cold Season* because of our film's purpose—ultimately saving us a boatload in rental fees.

If you still want to pursue borrowing gear, but rental companies aren't interested, consider approaching local colleges with film programs. You could either have students join your crew and check out their university's gear or speak to the faculty in the film department to get special permission. You'd be surprised how much film equipment universities have that sits around unused for most of the semester.

And borrowing isn't your only option.

Before purchasing any gear, write the manufacturer and pitch them your project. What's the worst that can happen? They make you pay full price? Several years ago, I had my eye on an expensive new rig. But before pulling the trigger, I decided to write the company and ask for special pricing.

What did I have to lose? Two days later, I found a heartfelt congratulations in my inbox, followed by a custom "JOSIAH20" coupon code that saved me nearly a grand.

All I did? Attach a cause and ask for help.

43| CAST AND CREW

Remember the filmmakers I surveyed about their struggles in the industry?

A prominent subset declared finding dedicated cast and crew members their number one concern. If you've ever produced a no-budget film, I'm sure you've also experienced the frustration of last-minute cancellations. I've had camera operators bail the day before the shoot. I've had cast members back out on the day.

Here too, FilmFuel provides solutions. From the start, this approach will make your film magnetic to the top talent in your area.

When you approach different actors, either through their agents, social media, or casting websites, mention the cause. "We're making this movie to benefit orphans," for example. Why? You want as many cast members as possible who identify with the cause and feel compelled to participate. My leads in *Orphaned Courage* didn't tell me until much later that adoption initially attracted them to the project. They identified with the cause and knew they had to join the effort.

When the going gets rough on set, the dedication of a cast who is all-in on the mission might just save the day. Because of a violent spring storm approaching the area, we had one less day at the warehouse location than anticipated. To compensate, we plowed through a sixteen-hour shoot day with the team's support. As we were nearing midnight, with two pages left to shoot, my team was ready to throw in the towel. And honestly, I wouldn't have blamed them. I was ready to quit! So, why didn't they leave? What kept them there? It was the cause. They took heart and carried on, motivated by something bigger than themselves.

"Come on. We can do this!" my team exhorted. I would never have planned a sixteen-hour shoot day. But if your back is against the wall and you've got no other option but to keep moving forward, a passionate team will help you maintain momentum.

With a cause behind your project, consider approaching up-and-coming actors in your region. These actors are given leading roles in many local films or have some star power to their name. Local celebrities or more established actors in your general vicinity will likely give you the time of day if your film has a charitable mission.

In the thirteenth chapter, I introduced the term "Actorvists" for big-name actors passionate about social causes. See if you can find *bankable actors* (those who would draw an audience) who are outspoken and passionate about the cause your film represents. Approaching these Actorvists is a long shot. But what do you have to lose? I never thought I would get ambulances, airplanes, and tactical vests in my films—but I did! All by asking.

If you reach out to an agent with a stunning project supported by a worthwhile charity their client is passionate about, who knows what could happen?

In Chapter 13, I also mentioned how friends of friends in the industry could help. If you have a "kinda" connection to an actor with star power, a project linked to a charity they're passionate about might be a winning way to connect with them.

How about finding a qualified crew willing to commit?

To be clear, never take advantage of people. Professional crew members who work on your production—sound, camera, lighting—aren't hobbyists.

This work is their livelihood. And goodwill doesn't pay bills.

However, besides raising funds to pay them using FilmFuel, a cause-driven film will also maintain their commitment throughout the project—and perhaps make them feel inclined to offer you a special rate because they believe in the project.

The secret? If they care about the cause, they'll stick around for the work.

Tell them a story about why they should care. The easiest way I've discovered to do this is to answer the question for yourself. As the director or producer, why do you care about this film? What does the cause mean to you? After you explain your connection to the mission, people typically discover a reason *they* can relate to the cause too.

Doing this helps your cast and crew catch your vision for the project.

Ultimately, I believe people want to be a part of something that lasts. If you can offer a positive working experience coupled with a cause they care about, you're golden. You'll have a quality team ready to rock.

44 | EXTRA, EXTRA!

In *Orphaned Courage*, we had several major crowd scenes. More specifically, we had several sports arena scenes that needed, at minimum, a few dozen extras. When working with a shoestring budget, how do you find large groups of people willing to come together to help you?

The first way I have had success is through churches. Even if your film isn't necessarily faith-based, it has a charitable cause, and churches will frequently want to get involved. Contact churches in the area, let them know what you're doing, and when you need people there. Frame it as a fun, exciting, one-of-a-kind group outing that will leave a lasting impact on others. I've been surprised by how supportive different congregations have been, rallying to support my projects.

Secondly, if you need a different demographic of extras, consider reaching out to fraternities and sororities on your local college campus. Many of these do charity work and are excited to volunteer for a meaningful cause. Campuses function as one giant network. So, if one organization on campus agrees, round up more people by having them invite their friends.

The third way involves incentivizing involvement. Get some gift cards, t-shirts, mugs, coffee beans—literally anything of value or interest—gifted by a local business. For example, one of our restaurant Fuelers was known for commonly giving out small gift cards as a promotion. Consider asking for a few dozen of these cards and either raffle them off or, if you have enough, give one to each extra after wrap.

As a side note, if you have a few gift cards left over, consider asking your Fueler if you can save them for later in the production—you never know when you'll need to bribe a noisy neighbor into postponing their lawn mowing.

Having some sort of door prize for extras who stick around until the end helps avoid volunteers leaving halfway through the shoot. Small gifts motivate the continued engagement and participation of the background actors.

A quick pro-tip: have a crew member focused on entertaining and exciting the crowd. I'm sure you've noticed lackluster extras in low-budget productions. That's what happens when it takes a half-hour longer to set up the lighting for a shot than a background extra expected. They lose interest and energy. Have someone check on the extras, give them a behind-the-scenes explanation, and get them some water—the role of a Second-Second Assistant Director on a larger set. This additional effort and the promise of door prizes will keep the experience fun and productive.

45| TELL ME WHAT YOU WANT

To sum up, keep the Fueler's desires in mind when making each approach, and you'll discover take-my-money kinds of support.

Who wants what? Businesses care about the return on their investment and the impact on their community. For these Fuelers, emphasize the advertising value of their participation (cha-ching!) and the film's social mission.

On the other hand, restaurants and caterers care more about the cause. Many are already familiar with contributing some of their products for promotional purposes. The unspoken question you need to answer for them? *Is this a good event to put our name behind?*

Locations care about exposure. *Will people know what location this is? Will more people come to my business because I'm letting you film here? Will the association with the film be a good one?* Emphasize the production's quality and your track record. In addition, highlight the value of having their logo in your film's credits. How many people will see their support and become aware of their venue?

Cast, crew, and extras care about the experience. They're likely wondering, *"Is this worth my time?"* Give attention to the work environment so that your team leaves your set with a positive impression. Improve the on-set experience with incentives, reasonable hours, quality meals, and a good vibe on set.

Before moving forward, take the time to revise your budget. Take into account the support businesses can provide at little to no cost. What are you spending your budget on currently? Which of those line items might be contributed to your project for free?

The next step is building a grand legacy event around the premiere of your film. You might be wondering if a launch event for your movie is necessary. *That sounds like a lot of work!* Here's the rub. Not only does a premiere build hype and credibility, but it's a milestone moment for a filmmaker. Even better, it makes your intangible impact visible so that everyone can see and appreciate your film's influence. It's a powerful experience that has the potential to be highly profitable for your cause and filmmaking career.

In Part 6, I will guide you through the process of organizing a massive premiere event that is sure to capture everyone's attention and become one of the most unforgettable nights of your life.

Ready to walk the red carpet?

I thought so.

» TAKE ACTION » » » » » » » »

☑ **Create a detailed budget breakdown for your project.** For now, assume you must pay in full for everything. Don't forget crew, catering, locations, transportation, and post-production costs.

☑ **Start applying budget cuts.** How can you apply what you learned in this section to secure some of these line items for little to nothing? Which of those could be contributed to your project? Who might be able to offer you those for free?

☑ **Plan out who you will approach for support and how.** Keep their different desires in mind and how you could frame your approach to address each. Businesses want a return on their investment and an impact on their community. Restaurants want to know about the supported charity. Locations want an increase in exposure. Your team wants a positive experience.

PART 6

WALK THE RED CARPET

46| WHY PREMIERE

"Hey Josiah, I just wanted to throw my hat in the ring and let you know that my production team and I have officially chosen a cause! We are finalizing plans for a legacy premiere this fall, which major TV networks have already expressed excitement to attend."

A few months ago, I awoke to see this brief email from a FilmFuel filmmaker in my inbox. After learning the system, this guy dutifully took the first steps and was now on the cusp of something incredible.

This section will show you everything you need to plan a highly anticipated, impactful, and profitable red-carpet premiere. It's a one-of-a-kind experience—the kind of moment you will remember forever. I still know people who consider the *Orphaned Courage Legacy Premiere* the greatest night of their life.

Buckle up. The following pages are your ultimate key to sustainable filmmaking.

Why is a premiere so valuable? First, *the build-up to a single event generates buzz and momentum around the launch of your film.* When a blockbuster makes it to theaters, it typically runs for several weeks. At the time of writing, the standard window for a theatrical release is 45 days—down from 90 before the pandemic. Still a month and a half!

Big studios have the print and advertising budget to keep people thinking about their films for a long time. Indie filmmakers don't. We've got one shot. Narrow your film's "release window" to a one-day event so you can give it everything you've got.

Premieres are also memorable. Chapter 45 discussed the importance of providing a quality experience for your team. That's true for fans as well! Who hasn't dreamt of walking the red carpet? Not only does a big event give people an excuse to have a good time, but the purpose of going— your cause—will stick with them long after the credits roll.

I'm also a big proponent of premieres because *very few are done well.* A genuinely unforgettable film event is a rarity. Not because it's so difficult to do, but because only a minority consider it worth the effort. Most filmmakers are so consumed with getting their movie to the finish line that they neglect the importance of a proper release. In most cases, the launch is an afterthought.

Indie flicks are rarely screened publicly outside of the festival circuit.

A final reason I think premieres are underrated is that they *validate the market potential of your film to distributors.* Think of your premiere as a pit-stop between post-production and distribution. An event is a proof of concept that your movie can turn heads. Getting hundreds of people to buy tickets to see your film puts you above the 90% of filmmakers who don't. Having that under your belt? Well, it might just make the difference between a distributor offering you a deal and taking a hard pass.*

Premieres are powerful. There's no doubt about it. And in the coming pages, you'll discover dozens of inventive ways to leverage an event into unparalleled momentum. Before I share examples from the premiere of *Orphaned Courage,* however, I want to make something abundantly clear.

I'm not saying I know it all.

Not even close.

Our premiere was a team effort of tedious trial and error. However, judging by the results, it's safe to say we stumbled across something fairly

---

* It's also worth noting that premieres encourage *repeat support* from Fuelers. If these business owners have a good experience, they will want to take part again. Once they see their logo promoted and a charity affected, they will know their money was well-spent and will be eager to be involved with your next film.

spectacular. Is it the only way to premiere your film? Of course not. But it is the best way I know. By using my team's discoveries as a blueprint for your releases, you can take the guesswork out of creating a successful premiere with a lasting impact.

Don't Launch at Festivals

You might be thinking, *"Wouldn't my debut festival appearance count as a premiere?"* And you'd be right. Technically, the first festival to publicly screen your film gets "premiere status" for your production.

However, because it's not your rodeo, you have little control over who comes or their experience once they get there. I have attended some incredible festivals, but I've also been to some clunkers. It's a gamble every time.

You can't be sure what films will be playing before or after yours, or what kind of audience will attend—*if* there will even be an audience. You won't really get a chance to announce your cause, and you definitely can't charge admission. Will you be honored with an award or sent home empty-handed? Who knows!

Film festivals present so many unknowns outside your control. These factors make it nearly impossible to generate a financial return or create a charitable impact. As many upsides as there are to festivals, they are ultimately no replacement for a premiere event of your own.

47| LEGACY PREMIERE 101

September 22, 2016, was a night for the books.

Let me set the stage for you. Our venue? The most luxurious theater in the city. The cast and crew arrived in lavish limousines. As soon as they stepped out onto the carpet, they were greeted by news cameras and fans. Everyone knew what a big deal this was.

Every legacy premiere will be structured a little differently. It comes down to your preferences and how you utilize your available resources. Although following the *Orphaned Courage* blueprint will likely create a similar experience, I invite you to go off-script and customize your premiere to your liking.

At the same time, if an idea I describe stands out to you, use it! As you're reading, circle anything you want to implement so you can refer to it when crafting your premiere.

Renting a Venue

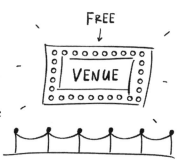

Location, location, location. It's a pivotal decision when buying a home—or hosting an event.

For most of cinema history, movies have been at home in theaters. And although there are many potential locations for your legacy event, there's something about hosting a red-carpet premiere in an actual theater that I would recommend to every FilmFuel filmmaker.

The hushed atmosphere.

The dimmed lights.

The crowd, buzzing with excitement.

There's nothing like the thrill of opening night.

Toward the end of the section, in Chapter 53, we will discuss alternative venue options. So, if a theater screening isn't feasible for your project or location, stick around.

If the only reason you haven't considered an event in the past is expensive rental costs, let me set your mind at ease. You have options. Our theater rental was paid for by a very generous Fueler who wanted to support the cause and a relative who starred in the film. Because of her kindness, we could spare more profits for charity.

However, with rental costs under a grand, it still could have been profitable to rent out the theater ourselves, had it been necessary. We would not only have recouped the rental fee but would *still* have had profits for charity. The point is, even if a venue comes with a hefty price tag, don't necessarily write it off as impossible. The right event can still be profitable.

Ticket Prices

Since we wanted the event to be perceived as exclusive and opulent, we priced our tickets accordingly. General Admission tickets went for $12.50, while VIP tickets were priced at $30 apiece. These VIP tickets included special seating, access to a backstage lounge, and the opportunity to network with the cast and crew after the screening.

The theater proprietor might as well have told us we were crazy, *"After a lifetime in this industry, I can safely say no one in Kentucky will show up to see a short film at those prices."*

But I was adamant that we could offer an experience to justify the premium price point. Unnerved by the proprietor's warning, however, I had no clue what kind of response we'd get.

By the night of our premiere, we had sold all fifty VIP and over six hundred General Admission tickets. Even at what some thought a prohibitive price point, people were willing to splurge and be a part of a grand, meaningful experience.

Side note—if your premiere is anything like ours, about 80% of ticket sales happen the week before the show. People are funny about committing to plans too far in advance. Even if you're promoting from the instant you announce the premiere, know that ticket sales may start as a trickle. Don't be disappointed or discouraged. It isn't a bad omen. Give the buzz some time to build. More on this later.

Also, keep in mind that the theater will take a cut of the ticket sales (in addition to the rental fee) if you decide to use their ticketing system. The benefit of using the theater's ticketing system is primarily convenience. In exchange for a cut of sales, the venue handles the ticket purchasing process—online and offline.

All ticket sales for your legacy premiere will feed into the box office numbers for the week, where the theater will tally up sales and write you a check for your portion. In most cases, I would recommend using the venue's ticketing system. Just be aware that the convenience will come at a small to moderate cost, off the top.

The Best of Times

While the date and time you select for your film's premiere may seem arbitrary, it is vital to the success of your event. If possible, host your event on a Thursday evening. Why?

Fridays, Saturdays, and Sundays are generally more expensive and mean competing with the launch of new studio blockbusters. Even if you can rent out a weekend screening at a multiplex, don't expect space in the main theater or a stunning turnout for your event. Weekday rentals are the way to go.

Monday, Tuesday, and Thursday are typically the least expensive rental days. My suggestion would be Thursday, as it's close enough to the weekend that many can take off work or free up their schedules to come.

How far in advance should I schedule my premiere? Give yourself a few months to get rolling. The extra time will make it possible to organize the logistics and fill seats. Our official red-carpet event that took place in late September started as a concept in mid-May. Four months may sound like a lot of time, but we were scrambling until the last second to get everything together. And that was with the help of a volunteer event planner.

For your premiere, consider the scope of the event first and reverse-engineer it. Is this something you need two weeks to plan? Two months? Then add a few days or a week buffer as contingency—something always goes sideways or gets delayed—and schedule the premiere accordingly.

48 | THE SETUP

Before people even made it *into* the theater, their luxurious experience began. We had an 8-foot by 8-foot step-and-repeat banner in the lobby covered in logos of the film and production company. In front of the backdrop, we placed a red-carpet runner.

As people waited for concessions in the lobby, we invited them to take pictures in front of the banner. Everyone loved the photo-op. At the same time, live jazz background music—contributed by a local musician—set the tone for an elegant evening.

The print shop that made our banner (a Fortune-50 brand) decided, because of our cause, to give us discounted pricing typically only offered to non-profits. Here again, the FilmFuel framework came in clutch.

Although the banner still cost a few hundred dollars to print, it was well worth the publicity. Fans who snap selfies will want to share them with their friends.

And share, they did.

Some friends *still* have profile pictures featuring the legacy premiere banner as a backdrop all these years later. In addition, every September, I see people sharing photos from the event as memories—with our logos prominently featured behind them.

This is a wonderful, grassroots way to build sustained attention. People scrolling through social media see the pictures and think, "*Orphaned*

Courage? What's that?" It spotlights your current film and keeps accruing publicity through your *next* release.

Bonus points if you decide to add your sponsor's logos to the step-and-repeat—remember from Chapter 45 what we said each Fueler wants out of their involvement? Placement on the banner could become a valuable selling point as you approach them for support.

Lobby Gift Shop

Also in the lobby were tables—a makeshift gift shop—to support the project and cause. There were special-edition t-shirts for sale and gift cards to download the film's soundtrack. Although the items we displayed were fun, this is an area I wish I had explored more. Unfortunately, we ran out of time, leaving money on the table. Don't make the same mistake.

Want to sell copies of your previous films? Set those out.

Want to sell stickers with your film's catchphrase? Amazing.

How about signed film posters? Yep—you can do that too!

The options are truly endless.

Remember that the best-selling items will always be meaningful gifts—things providing practical or emotional value—and not meaningless tchotchkes stamped with your logo.

Although our lobby efforts were limited, the event shirts were an instant favorite. Because of FilmFuel, the run was supplied at a discounted price by a local print shop. In addition, because of his connection to the cause, the print shop owner surprised us with dozens of other shirts as door prizes. Don't miss out on the opportunity of displaying meaningful gifts in the lobby. Done right, it will massively increase the profitability of your premiere.

Say Cheese!

Moments from your red-carpet debut will live rent-free in your head forever. At the same time, as the central cog in this massive event-engine, you'll be focused on a thousand tiny details, and time will fly by. Before you know it, the night will be over.

Do not underestimate the importance of getting professional photographers and videographers to document the event—for promotional purposes and reflection afterward.

From experience, I would say have two photographers at minimum.

One photographer should cover the step-and-repeat banner while the other gets candid shots. You've likely guessed by now that the two photographers at the *Orphaned Courage* premiere generously volunteered their time.

In retrospect, one of my biggest regrets is not getting a videographer to cover the event.

As filmmakers, we know how to find quality camera operators, right? That should have been the easy part! The no-brainer! Gratefully, some industry friends of mine vlogged their experience at the event and graciously sent me their footage. Whew.

Avoid this nerve-wracking oversight by arranging a videographer from the start. Have someone tasked with documenting this momentous occasion.

For many reasons, you'll be glad you did. The resulting highlight video not only reminds viewers why they came but becomes an important asset when you approach Fuelers for your next film. A highlight video of your premiere tangibly demonstrates impact.

A Grand Entrance

Which red-carpet premiere would be complete without an entrance from a limousine? Leading up to the event, the team enjoyed a pre-party at a producer's house nearby. The limousine then shuttled the cast and crew—a few at a time—to the theater so they could step out onto the red carpet in style. It's probably no surprise that the limousine service volunteered the ride because of a FilmFuel pitch, and rewarding our team with such a memorable experience made it even more special.

49 | AND SO IT BEGINS

Let's face it. The span between the doors opening and the show starting is boring. People have their concessions. They're comfortable in their seats and now must wait on you. Yawn.

Worse, long periods of aimless waiting can lead to frustration.

To remedy this, display a film-themed countdown screen to let your audience know when the screening will start. It gives them the freedom to "move about the cabin" if they need—to talk with a few friends or use the restroom—while ensuring they're back in time for the show.

One word of caution.

If you run a countdown screen, make sure you start the show when the timer reaches zero. We ran into a few technical issues at our premiere and decided to delay the show a few extra minutes to sort those out. The timer restarted, and some audience members who had arrived early and were tired of waiting understandably became agitated.

Don't make the same mistake I did. People will patiently wait if you tell them upfront how long they need to wait—but only if you keep your word.

The easiest way to create a compelling countdown is to edit some teaser clips of the film into a background loop behind the clock. Run the timer for the last fifteen minutes before the show and score it with a climactic portion of the film's soundtrack.

In addition, productively occupy your audience's time as they wait by placing special-event brochures in every seat. These might contain the film's title art, plot summary, featuring cast and crew, charity information, and the itinerary for the evening. On the reverse side, you can prominently advertise logos—and perhaps even special offers—from your Fuelers.

Introducing Your Film

After the countdown ends and the lights dim, the real fun begins. Here's where you get to introduce your film, thank everyone for showing their support, and do a little housekeeping.

Make this introductory speech entertaining and under ten minutes. Remember, people are here to see the film—not to hear you tell your life story. On the other hand, this is your moment in the limelight. If you made it this far, you've earned it. Enjoy every second. Walking out onto that stage and seeing all the people who showed up to support the team, my film, and our cause was mind-blowing. It felt like a rite of passage for me as a filmmaker—something I'll always be grateful for.

Sometimes it's easier to bring the house down if you have a co-host. Consider making your introductory speech a duet if you're a little nervous or want to amp up the energy in the room. Perhaps your co-host could be a recognizable local celebrity, key production partner, or lead actor in the film. My co-host, Eric Henninger, featured in the film as a sports announcer. And he killed it! If you'd like to see the exact script that Eric and I used to kick off the premiere, check out the book extras at **www.josiahstendel.com/filmfuelextras**.

Although I recommend memorizing your speech, having cue cards as a backup is never a bad idea. It's a big moment, and your mind will be in a million places. Imagine getting up there and freezing because you forgot your lines! Eek. These cue cards are lifesavers. Ours consisted of regular paper glued to half-sheets of black cardstock. The cardstock gave the cue cards an elegant look while remaining extremely practical.

The content and structure of the speech are up to you, but consider having everyone involved in the production stand as a way to honor them. Emphasize that although you may be the film's figurehead, you wouldn't be standing there if it weren't for them. Acknowledging your team's contribution is good form and goes a long way.

Now would be a great time to show some love to the Fuelers who made the project possible. Encourage your viewers to express appreciation by visiting their local establishments if they need X, Y, or Z. If representatives from your chosen charity made it to the premiere, invite them to stand and honor them for their work.

Next, I recommend doing some housekeeping. Tell your audience what to expect from the show—the much-anticipated screening, a question-and-answer session with the actors, and some door prizes.

It may sound weird but encourage your audience to keep their phones out. You don't want unnecessary distractions, but you *do* want your audience to take and share photos with the film's hashtag. Remember, every photo posted is a testimonial.

It's free publicity.

It helps build credibility, hype, and maybe even a little "fear of missing out" in the rest of the community. If you decide to throw an overflow event for those who missed out, they should feel like they *have* to come. We'll discuss this more later. Of course, you want viewers to focus on your film. But you also want to supercharge your marketing with free grassroots exposure.

50| ROLL FILM

This is it! Time to show off the work you and your team have put into the production.

Enjoy it. If you have a moment, look around during the screening. Look at the faces. Each one paid to be here. Notice those enraptured and entertained. Soak it in.

Surprise

As the credits rolled and the engineer brought the house lights back up, everyone rose to their feet. Never in a million years did I think we would receive a standing ovation for our simple little short film. As the thunderous applause died down, I took a sharp left.

"UNBEKNOWNST TO THE CAST AND CREW, I'VE PUT TOGETHER A BLOOPER REEL—"

The crowd suddenly ignited with murmurs.

"*So, as you guys enjoy the next five minutes, remember. This is the first time the cast and crew are seeing this too. Ought to be fun, right?*" A big groan escaped from the front row as my team realized what was coming. Everyone else in the auditorium laughed nervously in anticipation.

The surprise blooper reel that followed led to some of the evening's most hysterical and enjoyable moments. The point here isn't to put your team on blast but to enjoy some joviality together after a job well done.

Perhaps you don't have a blooper reel, or you think it wouldn't fit the mood of your event. You can do something similar with any other asset. You could share a behind-the-scenes featurette for your film or a teaser trailer for your next one. Get creative with it.

But do include a surprise of some kind to follow the film so people get even more than expected for the price of admission. Bonuses will keep your audience coming back for seconds.

Live Q&A Session

After the bloopers, we fetched a few key cast members for a question-and-answer session. At the same time, two runners with microphones fielded questions from the audience. Expect this to get deep quickly. Ours led to exciting conversations about personal connections to the cause, favorite roles the actors have played, or memories from production.

Going to a theater is traditionally a spectator sport, so give your audience a chance to warm up to the idea of speaking out.

One approach is to salt the audience with a few questions beforehand.

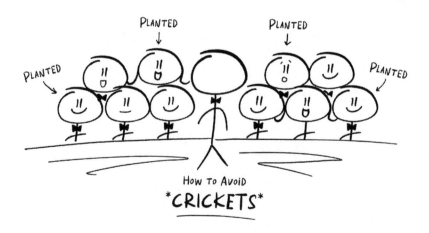

HOW TO AVOID
CRICKETS

For example, we asked some trustworthy friends to prepare some topics in advance. We instructed them to keep the session going by asking questions if no one else did.

This safety net removes the risk of awkward silence in spontaneous Q&A sessions. Once you get the ball rolling, others will likely contribute questions of their own.

They Get a Prize, and You Get a Prize

To incentivize attendance—and commitment throughout the program— we held drawings for door prizes at the end of the night. Some may leave the event early. That's normal. But anything you can do to keep the majority in their seats is worth it.

All the giveaways were contributed by dedicated Fuelers. They went above and beyond to provide beef jerky baskets, aromatic coffee beans, photobooks, service vouchers, clothing, gift cards, and more. Our film even inspired one artist from Poland to create a series of adoption-themed paintings, which he graciously donated to the premiere as door prizes. Giving away these exquisite works of art made the event even more memorable for our audience.

51 | PREPARE FOR AN ENCORE

Remember in Part 1 when I emphasized the value of a support system to propel your future projects? The best way to facilitate that scaffolding around you is to create **feedback cards** for your premiere.

Don't miss this.

To enter the giveaway, audience members filled out cards with their name, email address, a one-to-five-star rating of the film, and a few sentences of feedback. As expected, some only filled in their name to toss in for a chance to win. However, the door prizes motivated over four hundred of our six hundred audience members to thoroughly complete the cards and hand us their information.

This effort is vital because it lets you create an *email list* from your audience. The names and addresses of your fans are worth their weight in gold. Why?

They paid to be there.

If you were selling a product, they would be your customers.

And studies have shown it is *five times as expensive* to acquire new customers—viewers, in this case—than to keep existing ones. Said differently, getting your audience to return for another premiere is infinitely easier than assembling a new audience from scratch.

If you followed the previous steps and gave everybody in the room a night to remember, they're likely to come back for round two. Play your cards right, and you can already be building momentum for future projects before you've even finished this one. Do you see why this is so valuable?

Your audience is the key to repeated success. And an email list is the key to your audience.

Even if you haven't gotten anything else from this book, that single insight will pay for itself. The chance to get a list of your fans—those who are able and willing to support your projects—is invaluable. By the end of the premiere, my list included over four hundred people already invested in my work. They're the real deal. When I shared my next film with the same list, many were excited and supported me again.

Nurture this list to keep your viewers and create a career.

Remember *to comply with any relevant data privacy laws.* Include a statement on the card that declares your intentions with their information, such as "By filling out the card, you give us permission to reach out with film updates."

Of course, once you have permission to email them, don't be spammy.* Use the opportunity to connect with people who care about you and your projects. Perhaps by first sending a thank you note after the event and letting your audience know how much you were able to donate to charity because of their support. Later, remember this list as a starting point to launch and promote future films.

To save you some time, check out the template version of our feedback card in the book extras at **www.josiahstendel.com/filmfuelextras.**

In addition to the financial benefits of making a list, these responses provide truly insightful feedback. Not only will you collect dozens of snippets to share online as audience reviews, but you will also discover common gripes, such as starting on time, to remedy and elevate your next premiere.

---

* Make sure you include an "opt-out" function for those who want to escape your list.

End with Action

Most shoots begin with "Action!" However, as you wrap up the event, you want to end with action. Ask the audience to do something! Do you want them to take out their phones and subscribe to your YouTube channel? Rate the movie on IMDb? Or text their friends to see it?

Use the excitement of the evening to generate that action. Whatever your next step is, this can be your opportunity to grow a following and build anticipation for the future.

The VIP Experience

Following the close of the program, we hosted the sold-out VIP after-party. This is your chance to network with supporters, thank them for being there, and maybe even pitch a future project when you get asked what's next. It's time to gauge feedback from people who care about your work and are deeply invested in your success.

We had platters of hors d'oeuvres, live musicians, and Academy-Award-themed decorations in the lounge—all provided for free or at marginal expense because of the cause.

52| YOUR TURN

Now you're probably thinking, *Whoa—Josiah! Buddy! That's a lot! I have to do all that?* Nah. Pick and choose. Incorporate the attractions that make the most sense to you. In our case, we were screening a roughly 30-minute short film. I wanted to make sure attending the event would be worth the admission price and effort of coming in black-tie. If you're premiering a full-length feature film, it may be wise to streamline your itinerary.

Or come up with new activities! Perhaps you could crank up the drama and hand a representative from the charity an oversized check during your premiere. How fun would that be? One filmmaker followed up their short film by screening an old-school classic of the same genre. As long as legalities are squared away, that could be another possibility.

Can you turn your premiere into a haunted house? Just ask my dear friend and horror film maven, Antonio Pantoja. When he premiered his low-budget slasher flick, *One Must Fall,* he chose to craft the ultimate horror experience. Not only did he decorate the venue like the crime scene in his film, but he even hired some bit players to

205

skulk around in costume, scaring viewers silly. To say his audience enjoyed the thrill would be an understatement.

This is your chance to let your creativity run wild. Want a stand-up comedian at your comedy film screening? The only limit is your imagination. If you come up with something fun, I'd love to hear about it. Send your premiere story to the email address listed in Chapter 57.

If you'd like a complete breakdown of our premiere night, get a copy of the original event itinerary by visiting the book extras page at **www.josiahstendel.com/filmfuelextras**.

If you're feeling overwhelmed, instead of dismissing the idea of a premiere, consider involving a local event planner. We did. In an incredible twist, an actress in our film had extensive experience as an event planner and felt compelled to help us out. She was phenomenal.

Perhaps you can find someone willing to volunteer, as she did. But even if the event planner comes at a cost, they are worth every penny. Not a must-have, but keep in mind an event planner if all these options seem overwhelming.

I hope these examples demonstrated something important.

Did you notice how most items affected the event experience but not the expense? Fuelers generously provided otherwise pricey activities (a chauffeured limousine ride, for example) for free because of the event's charitable purpose.

Ask yourself what experience you want viewers to have.

What can you do to *enhance their experience at minimal expense?*

Dry Run

Do a complete run-through with the theater projectionist a few days before the event. This practice should be non-negotiable. You want to catch any bugs or glitches before the premiere. Your audience is paying a pretty penny to be there, right? Technical difficulties get in the way of a good experience.

Additionally, every theater differs in what they provide. Don't make assumptions. Maybe they'll have microphones, but what if they don't? For our introductory speech and actor Q&A session, we had to provide a public address system and microphones. These were generously brought and operated by a friend. Another yay for FilmFuel!

Ask lots of questions and explain your event's itinerary in detail to ensure everyone is on the same page. Lots of details, I know. But it'll be so worth the effort. If you go through with this, you'll have your community's attention, respect, and support.

53|
ALTERNATIVE VENUES

Let's say you can't access a theater. Maybe the only one in your area is a chain with policies restricting events. Or perhaps they're quoting exorbitant prices. Although theaters provide the most authentic cinema experience, the good news is alternative venues are plentiful. If you can't get access to a theater, give one of these a try.

The first substitute screening venue is a room at your local **library**.

Most public libraries have spaces you can reserve for free or rent inexpensively. Some rooms have projector screens and the ability to plug in your laptop. This makes a wonderful low-cost alternative for a modest film screening.

Secondly, consider premiering your film at a local **church**.

Even if your film isn't outspokenly Christian, having a charitable purpose opens up the potential of screening at local churches. Most modern church buildings have the infrastructure to handle a film premiere.

A third option is the auditorium of a local **school**.

I've seen several FilmFuel filmmakers have great success showing their films at schools. In this case, a weekend showing or screening during the summer may be the best way to avoid school functions and other commitments.

Similarly, a fourth alternative venue would be a **college auditorium**.

My grandmother, a respected author, screenwriter, and businesswoman, pioneered the FilmFuel approach I now champion. Back in the 1980s, as one of the first female members of Rotary International, she spearheaded a live comedy show where all the profits were donated to a local children's cancer research hospital. The nearby university opened its largest auditorium for free, and all the district's schoolchildren were invited. By putting a faith-based spin on the evening, she got local churches and Vacation Bible School programs to promote it. As you can imagine, the event was a roaring success.

In the same way, you could utilize local university auditoriums for your red-carpet premiere. Especially as a student filmmaker, these may be locations you get exclusive access to.

Our fifth alternative venue option is **hotels**.

Although perhaps unexpected, many prominent organizations host meetings, presentations, and conferences inside hotels. Most have a meeting area with a projector, much like library rooms. Some larger hotels even have convention spaces where tens of thousands can gather for trade shows and other events. None of these are off-limits. I'm still waiting for an email from a FilmFuel filmmaker who's able to fill a donated **sports arena** with fans for their latest film. It'll happen. I know it will. Maybe it'll be you?

The final alternative venue option is the ultimate low-budget solution.

Host your event under the stars **in a field** or as a **drive-in** movie. All you need is a screen, projector, PA system—and a field, of course—and you're well on your way.

These options all prove that you don't need a big theater for a memorable night. That being said, don't forget the audience experience. If you choose a humble location, go all-out in other areas. Have a red carpet, a step-and-repeat banner, live music, and t-shirts. Think outside the box, and you'll manage a wonderful time—and a massive return—at any venue.

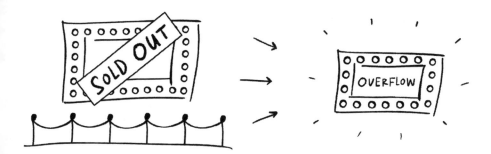

Overflow Event

If these alternative venues sound cool, but you would still prefer the theater experience, consider using one of these alternatives for an **overflow event**. There will be people who want to support you but who just can't make it the night of the premiere. Maybe they're traveling, working, or attending to a last-minute family situation.

With a low-key overflow event, you can offer an alternative screening for anybody who missed the first. And for those who loved the first screening so much they want to see the film again. Not to mention, it becomes another way to increase your profitability.

Don't try to make this an exact re-run of the main event. Different is okay. Keep it low-key and charge less for the meeker venue and experience. You might be surprised how many will come to both if given a chance. After our premiere, I had dozens of families wanting to know if the film would still be in theaters the next week so they could re-watch it with friends.

If you have an overflow screening planned ahead of time, you can even tee it up with all the buzz from the main event. Everybody who couldn't make it will have seen the pictures of the excitement they missed. Tell them via social media, "If you couldn't come last night, now is your chance! Grab some friends and come to the overflow event next week."

54 | HOW TO BE YOUR OWN HYPE MAN

By now, you should have a rough idea of what you could do with your premiere.

Perhaps you already see yourself stepping out onto the red carpet or snapping selfies in front of the step-and-repeat. But now, I'm sure you're asking yourself, *"How can I get the audience to show up?"* That's the $75,000 question.

On the night of our premiere, we hosted over six hundred raving fans. But they didn't show up by accident. We hustled *hard*. We wanted to be sure that people would be pouring in when those doors opened. And, boy—did they ever!

Heading into your premiere, I want you confident, too.

Our first step was old school. My producing partners and I hung up hundreds of **film-poster flyers** around town.*

We had a call to action at the top of each poster, inviting people to visit the movie website for tickets and more information. At the bottom, we

---

* Guess who got deep discounts on printing because of our charitable approach? Yes! I'm telling you—FilmFuel is magical.

had the event date, time, and venue. We hung these in every coffee shop, restaurant, bookstore, and business in town. In fact, we doubled back to all our filming locations and asked them to put up a flyer. We even offered an extra copy to put in their breakroom. Returning to Fuelers for premiere publicity shows the value of your support structure.

FilmFuel creates a pipeline to fast-track your funding *and* promotion.

Posting and messaging via social media also became a crucial component of ticket-selling. We created an event page and invited everyone we knew. Next, we had our cast and crew do the same. Four weeks, two weeks, and again a few days before, I messaged everyone who had engaged with the event a quick note: *"Excited that you might be coming to the premiere! How awesome! Just checking—have you had a chance to get your tickets yet? Only four weeks away, and we're expecting a full house!"*

Even if you're posting every few days with the link to buy tickets and you think you're driving everybody nuts, you won't believe how many times you'll hear, *"I totally forgot! Where can I get tickets?"* Some Fuelers have even had success inviting those who can't come to buy tickets anyway in support of the cause.

Press Forward

The FOX News anchor looked over at me—grinning from ear to ear.

"I've got a feeling you'll be back." As the *On Air* sign blinked off, I leaned over. *"I sure hope so."*

Everyone knows we live in a world of digital media. But traditional press outlets—newspaper articles and television coverage—can still do wonders for your ticket sales.

Why would they write about you?

When the Independent Critic reviewed my later short film, *The Cold Season*, there was something in his write-up that got my attention. "Although it should have a lasting significance for other aspiring filmmakers," he stated, "*The Cold Season* would be worth your time *for its noble mission alone*." Did you catch that? For the mission alone!

People care about the cause.

Outlets will give you airtime and column space *because* of the film's charitable purpose. It's a big deal if someone in Small-Town USA changes lives. That's headline-worthy! That's something people will read and watch.

I had the privilege of appearing on the local FOX and ABC news broadcasts to promote the upcoming red-carpet premiere. When I pitched the project on air, I shared not only the cause behind the film but also my personal motivation. I told them about my adopted cousins and my passion for making a difference in the lives of orphaned children.

In addition, I made sure to mention how the local community surrounded me with their support. Finally, I gave a brief call to action, inviting anyone interested to get their tickets and join us for the premiere.

Who do I reach out to at the newspaper or television station? Here's a brief cheat sheet of who you should contact when approaching traditional media.

For an article in your **local newspaper**, contact the editor. If your local newspaper is large enough, there may be multiple editors. In this case, contact either the editor of the entertainment section or the editor of the "local stories" portion of the paper. If there's an "inspirational stories" column, reach out to that section's editor. Once you know who you're looking for, their contact information should be readily available on the publication's website.

For **radio or TV**, connect with the station's news director. They curate the segment's stories and will decide if they would like to showcase you on an upcoming broadcast.

Be inventive as you search for unique avenues of media exposure. For example, a Fueler offered us the opportunity to show 30-second ads for *Orphaned Courage* on gas station pump screens in the days leading up to the premiere.

Electronic Press Kit

To prepare for press coverage, create an Electronic Press Kit (EPK) to send as a Zip file. Get in the habit of attaching this to your outreach emails so that any interested media outlets can find the information they need about your film.

Your press kit should include the following four items:

» Main EPK Info File
» Press Release
» Film Poster
» Production Stills

First, include a Main Info File PDF containing all your film's information. This document lists technical details like runtime and genre as well as short cast and crew biographies.* The Info File should end with any positive reviews or endorsements you received.

Next, include a press release and a PNG copy of your film poster. Round off your press kit with some production stills for these outlets to use in their write-ups.

If this is confusing or overwhelming, don't fret! Before I learned how all this worked, it seemed like a mystery to me. I had no idea what a science press release writing was! The good news? Our full EPK, info file template, and sample press releases are in the downloadable book extras to make this step as easy as filling in the blanks. Get started on your press kit by visiting www.josiahstendel.com/filmfuelextras.

Bloggers, Reviewers, and Podcasters—Oh My!

Your press kit can be used in many ways, including sending it as an attachment to film bloggers with a request for a review. To identify potential bloggers, I searched film reviews in my genre of choice. I clicked

---

* Use your filmmaking chops to your advantage. Instead of written bios, consider producing video interviews with each of your lead actors and department heads. These will stand out and become priceless assets you can include as links in your press kit.

through different film and YouTube channels to find those well-positioned to support my film with a meaningful review. Don't discount the little guys. When I reached out to the smaller outlets with a mention of the cause, I received a nearly 100% response rate.

Consider guest appearances on podcasts, too, not just in your industry or genre but in your area. Want to get booked as a guest on larger shows? Research previous guests and ask them for an introduction to the host. A deeper dive into film and event marketing is beyond the scope of this book. But the philosophy is simple. Figure out where your community goes to find local events. Find out where your audience is and *be visible there.*

In doing so, you will build a massive amount of hype around your premiere.

With FilmFuel, we received the venue, transportation, entertainment, advertising, photography, catering, door prizes, and so much more—for the cost of the time we spent asking. That's the big takeaway from these chapters. In *not* creating a premiere, filmmakers miss out on insane profit and impact. Don't shy away from this opportunity because of the effort required.

Go big. You'll be so glad you did.

In our final section, I want to take you to the real world and arm you with tricks to make the most of FilmFuel. Ultimately, this book shouldn't just give you a sugar rush. I want to make sure the FilmFuel method fundamentally shifts how you think about filmmaking and funding.

It truly changes everything.

» TAKE ACTION » » » » » » » »

First, choose a venue. Remember the options we explored in Chapters 47 and 53: movie theater (my top recommendation), library meeting room, church sanctuary, school or college auditorium, hotel meeting room, convention center space, sports arena, or outdoor drive-in location. Get in touch with local venues and explore all your options.

Next, create the itinerary. To get an idea of the scope, start mapping the itinerary around the evening's anchor piece—your film. Skim back through the chapters in this section. What elements of the *Orphaned Courage* premiere did you circle? Start listing out activities or amenities you could offer to increase the value of the event without significantly increasing the cost.

Reverse-engineer a release date. Much as you would with production, work backward to determine how long it will take to organize the logistics. After you have an estimated date, potentially several months in advance, allow up to a week extra as a buffer. Now you're ready to select the time and date for your premiere. Check with your cast and crew before booking to ensure they can be there. Remember, Thursday evenings often get the best results. Will you do an overflow event? If so, where and when?

Finally, start building buzz. Find film reviewers who can give advance endorsements of your project. Find podcasts that might have you on as a guest. Craft your press release and reach out for placement on local media outlets. Get creative and fill the house for your premiere night!

PART 7

PEDAL TO THE METAL

55 | PROFITABILITY HACKS

"Brilliant stuff. I'm already getting a ton of ideas! This whole approach has made me look at films in a different way. They're not just a form of entertainment, but a way to help people."

I hope you're in the same boat as the filmmaker who emailed me the above. You've learned the entire FilmFuel process from soup to nuts. The only step left is to put all the pieces together.

Maybe you feel like you've been drinking out of a firehose. *So much information, Josiah!*

All good. FilmFuel is an entirely new way of thinking about filmmaking. This book should be dog-eared, highlighted, and sticky-noted by the time you've finished your film. I want you to work through the *Take Action* sections and maybe even write ideas in the margins as you go back and apply each principle. If you

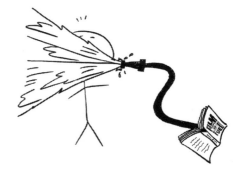

want to reference a high-level overview of the FilmFuel process, check out the end of this section.

This book is your map to sustainable filmmaking.

Go back and let it guide you through every step.

Before you ride off into the sunset, a happy and empowered filmmaker, let me leave you with some practical advice to apply FilmFuel in the most effective way possible. After your premiere, you're likely asking yourself what's next. Believe it or not, there are additional ways to build momentum and generate more fuel from the same film.

In the remaining pages, I want to show you three ways to do this.

The first strategy is to enter filmmaking **contests**. *Wait just a second, Josiah! I thought you didn't like contests! Isn't it like playing the lottery?* Well, kind of. Because the odds are never in your favor, contests are not a reliable way to raise funds. However, if your film is already in the can, contests can be a great way to get new eyeballs on your work. Let me explain.

Contests typically only allow you to submit work created during their entry window. So, for *Orphaned Courage*, we intentionally began principal photography during a top filmmaking contest. Of course, we couldn't enter the entire thirty-minute film, but we submitted an extended trailer—a three-minute featurette. For those eagerly anticipating the release of your movie, this sneak preview will crank their excitement to eleven. Although we placed in several categories, we fell short of taking home the grand prize. Instead, our win was the resulting publicity.

Many new fans and followers joined our social media channels. We received dozens of questions after the contest was over—from strangers—about the film's release date and future availability for purchase. As I learned, participation in contests can be an effective audience-building strategy.

The second avenue to post-premiere profit is **distribution**.

Discussing independent film distribution is also beyond the scope of this book. However, whether you decide to explore self-distribution or external distribution partners, don't let your premiere be the only time your film is seen. You'll leave a ton of cash on the table if you do. Your premiere is living proof that your film is commercially viable. If you get in touch with distributors, mention the premiere's results. Tell them how many showed up and how much money you generated for a worthy cause.

Ah, but Josiah, nobody wants to distribute short films. I thought the same! I had my sights set on sharing the film for free online when a filmmaker friend asked me why I hadn't considered shopping it around. With nothing to lose, I took the leap. And what a mistake bypassing distribution would have been! More than six years later, I *still* receive quarterly royalty checks for our humble, thirty-minute short film. And you can too.

Legitimate Distributors are Dealmakers.

It's a business.

If you can prove that your film—regardless of runtime—has the potential to make them money, they'll make you an offer.

Find other accomplished filmmakers in your genre and connect with them to get an inside track with these companies. Ask who distributed their films and what sort of experience they had. After building rapport and explaining the purpose behind your project, you could even ask for an introduction. You'll be surprised by the doors FilmFuel can open. I've personally done this for other filmmakers, and I think you'd be surprised at how many are willing to do the same.

The third and final profitability hack is your **email list.**

Following the premiere, you should have a list of at least one hundred people who are passionate about your work and willing to act in support. Use this list to your advantage. Judiciously.

Are the photos from the premiere available to see? Let them know.

Is your film out on DVD and VOD? Give them a chance to buy.

Have you released a new trailer? Ask them to share it with friends.

There are so many ways to keep your new fans engaged and excited about the impact they had. Perhaps you could share some statistics from the evening. How many people showed up in attendance? How much did you raise for charity? These are all announcements your fans want to hear.

If your film has an overflow event, ask them to come again and bring a friend. Will your flick be shown at a local film festival? Maybe you just won an award! That follow-up news story or critic review? Yes! Share that too. All these updates interest your supporters. Keep the conversation going to build anticipation for your next project.

Now, be careful with this. The most common mistake filmmakers make is not using their list at all. The second most common mistake is overusing their list. Be careful not to go overboard with emails, or you'll start seeing people unsubscribe from your list. My rule of thumb? An email every two or three weeks—no more. You can ramp up as you get closer to your next film. For now, get in touch often enough that they don't forget about you, but seldom enough that they don't get annoyed.

Keep it special.

Tax Benefits

Although FilmFuel already benefits you by attracting resources and creating change for others, there's one final benefit we have yet to discuss. Taxes. Whenever profits come into your production business, taxes go back out, right?

When you contribute to the charity after your premiere, that donation is tax-deductible—offsetting the profits from your film premiere and potentially lowering the amount of tax you are required to pay.

Your CPA can explain this better than I can. The bottom line is that the actual donation to charity will also benefit your production company by lowering your tax liability. Wahoo for FilmFuel!

56| BIGGER BUDGETS

Over the years, I've gotten several questions from FilmFuel filmmakers about how to apply this process to seven- or even eight-figure budgets. It's not impossible, but it does require another mindset shift. If you want to raise millions of dollars, consider *tag-teaming* FilmFuel with a traditional funding strategy. Funding methods are not mutually exclusive. In fact, blockbuster budgets are typically made up of funding from a variety of sources.

For example, finding backers is way easier if your Kickstarter campaign has a FilmFuel cause attached. FilmFuel dramatically increases your chances of being awarded a grant. Do you think there are big-name producers out there who care about causes? You know it. Although FilmFuel works solo, it can also act as a momentum multiplier when attached to any old-school funding method.

Secondly, if this is your first-ever film, I recommend a budget no higher than $10,000.

Let me put that into context. Remember what you're offering Fuelers. You're giving them advertising exposure. If this is your first rodeo, how much is an advertisement in your credits worth? Because of the film's purpose, Fuelers will still contribute in blind faith. However, *expect smaller increments*. Initially, you might be able to request $200 to $500 in exchange for a company's logo in your credits.

That *will* add up quickly.

But if you're attempting to raise a $4 million budget?

Oof! Insanely tedious.

Remember, think long-term. Will this be your last film? I didn't think so.

Keep a modest first budget and focus on building your support structure. Prove you can make it work. Then you will have evidence to show the next time you approach these businesses. By proving profitability, you will show Fuelers the value of having their logo in the credits, on the premiere banner, or on the back of a t-shirt.

At that point, you can start expecting higher levels of support from each business. Eventually, you'll have the credibility to expect $10,000 or more from each logo placement. Why so much? Because your advertisements will be worth that much to them. Instead of thousands of small contributions, you'll only need a few larger ones to fund that multi-million-dollar dream project.

Customer-Audience Overlap (Advanced)

The secret of FilmFuel is *alignment*. Alignment between cause and plot. Alignment between cause and self. And—for bigger budgets—alignment between plot and Fuelers.

In Chapter 18, I suggested finding Fuelers related to your story. For example, you could approach theme parks to fund an action flick, gun ranges to fund a war film, or escape rooms to fund a thriller. But this technique is more than a guidepost on the way to finding Fuelers. This advanced technique is the key to bigger budgets.

The amount you charge Fuelers for advertising in the credits is directly proportional to the *value* you offer in exchange. What value do Fuelers get in exchange for partnering with you? Remember the Third Win—an advertising write-off. What's the goal? That viewers buy their products and services.

By searching for Customer-Audience Overlap, you *increase the value* of your offer by increasing the likelihood that viewers buy from your Fuelers.

Put yourself in their shoes. Imagine you own an escape room. You offer an immersive experience where participants are locked in a themed room and must solve riddles to escape in time. What kind of people are your customers? Maybe people who enjoy brain-teasers, puzzles, and problem-solving—the thrill of a ticking clock and the mental challenge presented to them. What movies would your customer watch? Probably films with mystery elements and brain-bending plot twists, like thrillers.

That means thriller film viewers have a lot in common with your customers. There's alignment. If you could advertise your escape room in front of that audience, there's a better chance they would become customers than if you advertised in front of, say, comedy film viewers.

You would *pay more* to get your logo in front of a thriller audience because there's more overlap and a better chance they will be interested in your product.

Because there's a better chance you will profit, it's more valuable to you.

Because it's more valuable to you, you're willing to pay more.

Do you see where I'm going with this? If you can identify businesses whose customer base overlaps with your film's audience, you can leverage this in your pitch and charge two to ten times more for the *exact same offer.*[*]

Find as many Fuelers as possible with Customer-Audience Overlap and watch the funding roll in. Romance films could partner with spa resorts, flower shops, fine dining restaurants, or dating services. Science fiction

---

[*] When you pitch Fuelers aligned with your film's plot, be sure to highlight the similarities between their customer base and your target audience. This will demonstrate the added value they stand to gain from funding your film. It's a big selling point.

films could collaborate with tech companies, space-themed amusement parks, or virtual reality experiences. Sports movies could pitch gyms, sporting goods stores, and even sports teams for sponsorship.

Same pitch. Same offer.

Different *value*.

Resulting in *more funds—faster*.

57 | WHAT NOW

At this point in nearly every non-fiction book, the author pulls a subtle bait-and-switch. Contrary to what they've said all along ("Anyone can do this!"), they tell you it's too challenging, expensive, or time-consuming to do on your own. Then, they'll offer you a high-ticket masterclass, inner circle, or coaching deal to get results faster. Although I think most of these authors are genuinely trying to help, it feels like a money grab to me.

I respect the hustle, but this book is different.

There's no sales pitch here.

There's no gotcha, upsell, or operators standing by.

From cover to cover, my sole intent has been to help you.

My hope—the reason I wrote this—is to demystify the film funding process. You now know how to find a cause that fits your film. You've been armed with the tools to pitch Fuelers and fund your film on your own terms. You've discovered tricks to maximize your budget with resources you never thought you had access to. Best of all, you've got the blueprint to a massively successful red-carpet legacy premiere in your hands. Creating a world-changing event around your world-changing film is now simply a process of following the steps and filling in the blanks.

The only question left is, *will you?*

I told you at the start that there are only two kinds of people in this industry. Those who take action and those who talk about it. Those who turn movies into movements with FilmFuel and those who wait for their big break. You can't be both.

The downward spiral of excuses is the path of least resistance, but it will take you nowhere. You've got all the tools to greenlight your project now. Everything you need is in this book. The answer is literally in your hands!

And if you need help along the way, you've got someone in your corner now. Shoot me an email,* and I'll be happy to help you get unstuck.

Attaching a cause is everything. It's the life-changing film funding secret—the lifeblood of turning a profit with your indie film, and more importantly, the key to changing lives with the art you create. Powering films by empowering others. It's what FilmFuel is all about.

If you're still waiting on a mythical investor to swoop in and save the day, I've got news for you. The cavalry isn't coming. I'm sorry. And as I hope you can see now, that's a good thing.

Now it's your turn to take action, fund your film, and change lives.

---

* Get in touch by emailing me@josiahstendel.com. I'm always there to help and support you.

» TAKE ACTION » » » » » » » »

- **Find a cause motivated by your story** by starting with your film's moral premise.

- **Select your charity** using a combination of the *FilmFuel Assessment*, search results, local opportunities, and Fourth Wall Causes.

- **Reach out to the charity** and tell them what you're doing to build a relationship. Be sure to request a list of businesses that sponsor them.

- **Choose your monetization model**. Are you going to donate all the profits or a percentage?

- **Find businesses** from the list supplied by your charity, your personal connections, and your network contacts.

- **Approach each business** on sunny Fridays, emphasizing the Third Win.

- **Make sure you bring** your sponsor One-Sheet, proof of concept trailer, budget breakdown, and other assets that might spark imaginations and excite Fuelers about your film.

- **Approach your friends** with a similar Quick Pitch. Ask them to connect you with business owners in their network who might be interested in supporting you.

- **Repeat your pitch** to restaurants and other entities that could help you in other ways—craft services, locations, equipment, etc.

- **Build a luxurious legacy premiere** that gives your fans a night to remember—with step-and-repeat banner, limousine, countdown timer, thank you speech, the film itself, a surprise blooper reel, live question-and-answer session, door prizes, call to action, and an epic VIP after-party.

- **Build hype** before the premiere with TV, newspaper, and other online press outlets.

- **Donate the allotted profits** to the charity! Make this a big moment if you can—with the oversized check and everything. This is the final payoff for your project.

- **Generate further profit** by participating in contests, securing distribution, and building an email list to empower your future projects.

- **Rinse and repeat** for your next film, gradually ascending into bigger and better budgets.

AUTHOR'S NOTE

As we turn your movie into a movement, let me lead by example.

A portion of the profits from this book will go to charity—with a twist. *You get to pick which one!* Just visit **www.josiahstendel.com/filmfuelextras** and choose the cause that speaks to you. Ten seconds or less to change someone's life forever. Fair deal?

Look at you—haven't even had a chance to implement FilmFuel yet and you're already making a difference! Feels good, right? I promise this is just the beginning.

To your success,

ACKNOWLEDGMENTS

Creation is collaboration. Much like a director gets the credit for the combined effort of his team, the author is often the only one celebrated for writing a book. But if we're honest, FilmFuel would never have happened without the involvement of countless others.

I would first like to thank my beautiful wife, Bethany, who played every supporting role imaginable on this project and sacrificed much of her own time so I could write. Thank you for nurturing my wild ideas and for inspiring my creativity.

Thank you to the rest of my wonderful family—Eden, Mom, Dad, Sarah, Christa, Danielle, Jeremiah, Shavonn, Jeremy, and Caleb—for letting me workshop ideas in their company. This book would never have happened without you as my collective sounding board.

To my first victims—er, actors I had the privilege of directing: Silvio Wolf Busch, John Wells, Chad Zigmund, Shelby Taylor Mullins, Clint Calvert, Eric Henninger, Perry Mains, and more—thank you for giving a then sixteen-year-old kid a chance and for believing in him as much as he believed in you. Because of our *Orphaned Courage* adventure, I have become better at shepherding great talent to make great art. Thank you for that. Despite my inexperience, we still somehow stumbled into impact.

To my first Fuelers—the ones who contributed to *Orphaned Courage* and all my projects since. Thank you for seeing potential in me worth investing in. I owe you a debt of gratitude.

To my OG FilmFuel filmmakers—Christopher Shawn Shaw, Susan Shearer, Jamie Hope, Luis Hindman, Scott Peterson, Stephen Hunter, Don McLennan, Afroz Khan, Jake Starkey, and Mike Wech—thank you for the opportunity to consult on your projects and for the invaluable feedback that enabled my ideas to transcend genre and geography. You guys believed in this framework before it was cool. I can't thank you enough.

I'll always be grateful to Ryan Connolly and the Film Riot crew for being my film school. Without the time and effort you put into educating a generation of filmmakers, I would probably be building robots. Which I guess would be cooler and make me more money, come to think of it, but what I'm *trying* to say is that I wouldn't be a filmmaker if it weren't for you—I'm grateful.

To Jeremy White and Kendra Knox— thank you for helping me find my footing in this industry. Before starting anything, I revisit every brilliant note and piece of advice you gave me. Not only has your encouragement made me a better storyteller, but I can trace back my passion for filmmaking to the set of *Summer Snow*. Thank you for investing in me.

To Dr. Judy Spain, J.D., CCEP—you told your class you would always be willing to help as long as it didn't require visiting us in jail. (You're not that kind of lawyer.) Because of your help, that should never be necessary. Thank you for reviewing my manuscript for legal potholes.

The secret to creating something great—whether book or film—is to surround yourself with people smarter than you. I want to honor the wisdom of those people whose advice and support carried me to the finish line: Elliot and Zander Weaver (love you both), Luke Thompson and Rodolphe Pierre-Louis (can't believe we met on Kickstarter), Mark and Jay Duplass, Noam Kroll, Darius Britt, Dustin Lee, Aviv Vana, Antonio Pantoja, Josh Stifter, Gino Wickman, Jay Steinfeld, Akshay Nanavati, Kenneth Frank & In the Garage Productions, Johnny Catalano, Bill Rosenthal, and Chad Cogdill.

To Yago Domingues—obrigado, my friend! Thank you for the beautiful cover. There's something tangibly special about your art. Please raise your prices for everyone but me. Não se subestime.

To Dallas Jenkins, Derral Eves, and the rest of the amazing team at *The Chosen*—it's an honor to stand shoulder-to-shoulder with you. Thank you for helping me realize how much my work can impact others and for the front-row seat at seeing some of my pet theories in action. You've inspired me to bring my loaves and fish and leave the impossible math to God.

ACKNOWLEDGMENTS

Finally, I thank you. Life is short, and time is precious. I hope I gave you something valuable in return for some of yours. Now go. Be fearless, fuel your film, and let nothing stop you from making your movie a movement.

That's a wrap, guys.

APPENDIX

CAUSE RECOMMENDATIONS BY GENRE

Use this as a quick reference to get you thinking in the right direction. For a more detailed, interactive version, check out the *FilmFuel Assessment* on the book extras website—**www.josiahstendel.com/filmfuelextras**.

Documentaries

These films cover a wide range of topics and themes. The right choice will, in large part, depend upon the focus of your documentary.

FOR DOCUMENTARIES ABOUT...

» Climate change, endangered species, or the natural habitats of wild animals—try connecting your film with environmental conservation charities.

» Human rights violations, inequality, or discrimination of some kind—try a charity dedicated to the social justice issue in focus.

» Education reform or access to education—consider partnering with a charity improving education or building schools in developing countries.

» Medical breakthroughs, public health crises, or healthcare disparities—try medical or healthcare charities.

» Artists, musicians, or specific cultural events—consider a non-profit that supports the arts or improves the lives of others through art.

» Animal rights, wildlife conservation, or animal rescue—try charities focused on animal welfare.

» Natural disasters, a humanitarian crisis, or an emergency response effort—try disaster relief charities.

» Community activism, grassroots organizations, or urban renewal efforts—consider charities focused on community development, affordable housing, or revitalizing low-income areas.

Narrative Genres

ADVENTURE, TRAVEL

» Charities that protect or restore endangered wildlife in the part of the world your film takes place in.

» Charities that deal with dangerous environments or situations— like those that provide free surgical care to the poorest nations.

» High-octane or high-stakes organizations that mirror the adventure in your film. For example, disaster-response charities that deploy volunteers into critical disaster zones.

CRIME, MYSTERY

» Charities dedicated to giving the wrongfully accused a second chance—especially if your film has a plot twist.

» Charities that support local law enforcement or the families of fallen officers.

» Charities that reach incarcerated individuals or those that work to reintegrate former inmates into society.

» Charities related to the cause of death (ex. gun violence) or victim.

» Charities working to end homelessness—especially if your film features crime on the streets.

DISASTER, SURVIVAL

» Charities that offer disaster relief, perhaps linked to the disaster (fire, flood, tornado, drought, etc.) in your film.

» Charities that support general survival. For example, charities bringing clean drinking water to those without it.

» Charities that protect or restore endangered wildlife.

» Charities that deal with dangerous environments or situations—like those that provide free surgical care to the poorest nations.

WAR

» Charities that provide disabled military veterans with support.

» Charities that support veteran-owned businesses or provide financial assistance to entrepreneurial veterans.

» Charities devoted to the treatment of Post-Traumatic Stress Disorder (PTSD) in veterans.

» Charities that preserve the history of a specific war to honor those who lost their lives fighting in it.

» Charities that provide education, protection, and support to children affected by conflict.

» Charities founded by veterans, like those deploying retired soldiers to help recover children kidnapped into human sex trafficking.

WESTERN

» Charities that allow children to experience the Old West.

» Charities that protect wild horses and burros in the American West.

» If your film features Native American culture, history, and people, consider charities that provide scholarships for Native American students pursuing higher education.

» Charities that focus on the same good-versus-evil themes of Western films—such as those deploying retired soldiers to help recover children kidnapped into human sex trafficking.

» Charities that provide financial assistance to injured and disabled rodeo athletes.

SUPERHERO

» Charities that recruit volunteer superheroes to visit sick children in hospitals.

» Charities that fight for social justice and equality in different arenas—whether for immigrants, racial equality, or the representation of some other underprivileged minority.

» Charities founded by real heroes, like those that send retired soldiers to help recover kidnapped children.

» Charities that support humanitarian efforts overseas.

» Charities related to the comic book or superhero movie industry like those for comic book creators in need and those founded in honor of superhero actors like Christopher Reeve and comic book writers like Stan Lee.

COMEDY

» Charities that use comedy and entertainment in therapeutic applications.

» Charities related to smiling like those that perform cleft lip and palate surgeries to restore the smiles of children in need.

» Charities related to using laughter as a healthcare cure.

» Charities that provide a "safety net" for comedians in need.

» Charities that fund cancer research and treatment through comedy events.

ROMANCE

» Charities that provide weddings for couples facing terminal illnesses.

» Charities that provide couples counseling, work to end relationship abuse, and support healthy relationships.

» Charities that provide resources and crisis support for unplanned pregnancies.

» Charities that focus on reuniting refugee families and restoring broken homes.

» Charities that deploy retired soldiers to help recover children kidnapped into human sex trafficking.

SLASHER/GORE

» Charities that support survivors of violent crimes, domestic abuse, or trauma.

» Non-profits focused on suicide prevention and crisis intervention.

» Mental health charities that help trauma and PTSD victims.

» Heart-health or blood-related healthcare organizations.

» Psychological Thriller

» Mental health charities that help trauma and PTSD victims.

» Mental health organizations using art as an intervention.

» Charities that support survivors of violent crimes, domestic abuse, or trauma, since many films in this genre address those themes.

» Non-profits focused on suicide prevention and crisis intervention.

» Heart-health organizations.

» Anti-human trafficking charities, even—anything that you can connect to the mental or physical turmoil of your characters.

MONSTER

» Anti-bullying charities that empower youth to stand up against bullying and promote inclusion in their communities.

» Charities working to making hospitals less scary for children.

» Charities providing free Halloween costumes to children in need.

» If your film features a whale, shark, or another big animal as the monster, wildlife protection charities.

PARANORMAL

» Charities honoring the deceased such as those creating and maintaining memorials for cyclists killed riding on public roads.

» Charities providing support for children and families dealing with the grief of a loss.

» Charities working to make hospitals less scary for kids.

» Charities providing free Halloween costumes to children in need.

COMING OF AGE

» Charities focused on youth development, such as those matching adult mentors with youth facing adversity or those providing agriculture, STEM, and civic engagement opportunities for kids.

» Organizations with a focus on supporting arts in schools.

» Non-profits with an emphasis on education—whether providing schools with supplies they need or those building schools in developing nations.

» Charities supporting children in low-income areas.

» Anti-bullying and anti-cyberbullying organizations that bring attention to the damage bullying can cause and provide solutions for more inclusive classrooms.

» Opportunity-providing charities that develop financial literacy and entrepreneurship skills in youth.

FAITH-BASED/FAMILY

Films in this genre can partner with pretty much any charity. However, the closer it connects to your story, the more meaningful and powerful it will be.

» Charities focused on family development, such as those matching adult mentors with youth facing adversity or those providing agriculture, STEM, and civic engagement opportunities for kids.

» Non-profits with an emphasis on education—whether providing schools with supplies they need or those building schools in developing nations.

» Charities reuniting refugee families and restoring broken homes.

» Adoption assistance funds which provide interest-free loans to families interested in adoption.

» Charities supporting families and children in low-income areas with affordable housing or community revitalization efforts.

» Charities that provide weddings for couples facing terminal illnesses.

» Anti-bullying and anti-cyberbullying organizations that bring attention to the damage bullying can cause and provide solutions for more inclusive classrooms.

» Opportunity-providing charities that develop financial literacy and entrepreneurship skills in youth.

» Charities that provide family counseling or organizations that focus on ending relationship abuse and supporting healthy relationships.

» Charities providing resources and crisis support for unplanned pregnancies.

» Charities that deploy retired soldiers to recover children kidnapped into human sex trafficking.

» Faith-based non-profits and ministries that provide aid to the poor and ill in Jesus' name.

SCIENCE FICTION—SPACE/ALIENS

» Space exploration charities that fund space-related projects and research.

» Charities that promote astronomy education by donating telescopes or providing a variety of educational programs.

» Space-age charities focused on protecting humanity. For example, those conducting research on asteroid detection and deflection, with the goal of protecting Earth from asteroid impacts.

» Space travel non-profits that aim to democratize space travel by sending ordinary citizens to space.

» Space investment organizations that empower entrepreneurial space ventures, space settlement, and space-based solar power initiatives.

» Charities that encourage young people to become leaders in space-related fields.

» Charities that seek to close the gender gap in technology fields, if your film is high-tech or features a female protagonist or supporting character.

» Science Fiction—Dystopian

» Disaster relief or emergency preparedness charities, since many movies in this genre depict societies raved by some form of disaster or epidemic.

» Hunger relief non-profits since access to food and clean water becomes a major concern in a post-apocalyptic world.

» Environmental charities if your film is set in a damaged or decaying world.

» Mental health charities helping trauma and PTSD victims.

» Suicide prevention and crisis intervention charities.

SCIENCE FICTION—ROBOTS/ADVANCED TECHNOLOGY

» Charities that encourage young people to pursue a career in a STEM field.

» Charities related to robotics advances in healthcare.

» Charities that use technology to improve the world. For example, some charities solicit engineers to volunteer time and expertise to help communities in need across the globe. Others use cutting-edge tech to remove pollutants from the ocean.

» Organizations that improve education and technology access for children in developing countries.

» Non-profits that empower citizens to contribute to important scientific discoveries.

SCIENCE FICTION—TIME TRAVEL

This genre can be tricky to connect closely with a cause, so let's think outside the box and link your film to the broader themes of time, memory, and preserving history.

» Charities fighting against Alzheimer's which messes with memory and perceptions of the past.

» Charities that alter the future of a community like those which bring clean and safe drinking water to people in developing countries.

» Charities investing in future generations, like those encouraging young people to pursue a career in a STEM field or those that seek to close the gender gap in technology fields.

» Charities that fund research and projects related to the theoretical possibility of time travel.

» Charities that preserve key moments and movements in our history for future generations.

FANTASY

» Animal welfare organizations that work to prevent animal cruelty or to protect endangered species and their habitats—since many fantasy movies feature mythical creatures or talking animals.

» Environmental conservation charities—since fantasy worlds often depict nature in a magical and mystical way.

» Charities in support of human rights and quality—since films in this genre often deal with themes of oppression and social justice.

» Charities that develop imagination and creativity in youth.

CAUSE RECOMMENDATIONS BY MORAL THEME

Discussing every moral premise is beyond the scope of this book. However, these are five of the most common moral themes found in films and some potential charity connections for each.

1. Good triumphs over evil: One of the most common moral premises is the idea that good will eventually triumph over evil—no matter how dark it may seem now, justice will prevail in the end! This theme is present across genres, from action movies to dramas and even comedies. Three charity "paths" related to this theme could be...

» Charities that exonerate wrongly convicted individuals, giving them a second chance.

» Charities that rescue victims of violence, exploitation, and modern-day slavery and bring their perpetrators to justice.

» Charities advocating for girls' education and empowering young women to become community leaders.

2. Redemption and second chances: Another common moral theme is the idea that people can change, even after making terrible mistakes. In films, this often involves characters being given a second chance at life or making amends for their past. Three causes related to this theme could be...

» Charities that exonerate the wrongly convicted. This one is a repeat, but since these charities give wrongly convicted felons a second chance, this also fits here.

» Charities that provide employment, education, and other resources to help those with a history of homelessness, incarceration, and substance abuse to rebuild their lives.

» Charities that build and repair affordable housing for families in need, giving them a fresh start and a chance at a better future.

3. Love conquers all: Love can overcome the most difficult obstacles. Many films explore this theme through stories of romance and sacrifice. Three causes related to this theme could be...

» Charities that grant wishes to children with critical illnesses, bringing them hope, strength, and joy during difficult times.

» Charities that provide weddings for couples facing terminal illnesses.

» Charities that deploy retired soldiers to help recover children kidnapped into human sex trafficking.

4. The importance of family and community: Films often emphasize the ways in which relationships can provide support and comfort during difficult times.

» Charities that match youth with adult mentors serving as positive role models that offer support and guidance.

» Charities focused on restoring broken homes by reuniting refugee families across the globe.

» Charities providing housing and support for families of seriously ill children who must receive medical treatment far away from home.

5. The human condition: Finally, many films explore the complexities of the human experience. This includes themes of mortality, the search for meaning, and the struggle to find your place in the world. This theme can be found in nearly every genre—from dramas to science fiction and even fantasy films.

» Charities that help trauma and PTSD victims.

» Suicide prevention and crisis intervention charities.

» Charities funding research, providing patient support, and advocating for cancer prevention and early detection.

» By necessity, these are broad and generic strokes. Please take the time to drill down into your film's specific moral themes by following the framework in Part 2 of this book.